Hazel Butterfield is a presenter, blogger and book enthusiast originally from the North and has been loving living in South West London for the last 20 years. Presenting on radio and TV, she is known for her quirky attitude and fiery nature. Her degree in psychology and passion for mental well-being issues are a key focus for discussions in her book show 'Get Booked' at WRS womensradiostation.com/get-booked/ as well as her weekly SW London based show 'Riverside Today' at Riverside Radio www.riversideradio.com/shows/riverside-today-with-hazel. You can find her blog at HazelButterfield.com covering anything and everything, especially her passion for reading, eating, and well-being.

To my children and my dog. My favourite people, most of the time.

Hazel Butterfield

20 WEEKS

AUSTIN MACAULEY PUBLISHERS™

LONDON • CAMBRIDGE • NEW YORK • SHARJAH

A CIP catalogue record for this title is available from the British Library.

ISBN 9781398494053 (Paperback)
ISBN 9781398494060 (ePub e-book)

www.austinmacauley.com

First Published 2023
Austin Macauley Publishers Ltd®
1 Canada Square
Canary Wharf
London
E14 5AA

Where do I start? I could in theory thank anyone that contributed to my need for such intense therapy, because it was invaluable. Or maybe just the ones who stood by me while I rebuilt myself after imploding. I truly regard myself as having the best and most bonkers of friends that take camaraderie, honesty, joy and a sense of belonging to a new level.

I have to and want to also thank my children for giving me permission to publish this book and for being quite exceptional. You're both weirdly delicious, funny and wonderful.

Table of Contents

Introduction

The title of this book evolved so many times as I went through the writing process. Going through the counselling, it helped me realise and work through many issues I was dealing with. But actually writing about it, the cathartic nature was so incredible in that it help me to realise so much more about myself. Things that possibly I wasn't even too aware of when I was discussing it with my counsellor, affording for the reflective time. And therefore there were so many different titles that fit. Here are just a few...

20 weeks – Headstrong – Everybody Lies – You know what I mean?

Where do I start? The beginning seems like such a cliché. So maybe I'll start with right now and then bounce around as I go along.

I'm sitting in bed, it 3.26am and I've been awake for at least an hour. I've tried distracting my mind with mundanity so that it doesn't wander into territory that will occupy my mind like the plague. Feasting on insecurities, scenarios, reality and outright idiocy – that's not going to send me back to sleep. Thinking about my work outfit for tomorrow or packed lunch ideas, will. Because it's dull. It's like training the brain, it will wander but keep at it. At least making sure I have a plan in the morning is productive, it saves time. Anything that goes through your head at 3am is absolute bollocks, it's not real, and it's darkness dialogue.

I've always felt like I was on the edge. I guess that's why I became the coping strategy queen, until it all came crashing down. Monumentally. There is only so much you can handle.

I felt irrelevant. My feelings, what happens to me, was irrelevant. I felt incredibly let down. "Oh it's Hazel, she'll be fine." News flash – I wasn't.

I always had a sneaky suspicion that nobody gave a shit so to avoid knowing, or disappointment I made sure I didn't need to find out. Until I did find out regardless! I guess you can't always run from your fears. Do you know when you have anxiety dreams about crazy situations that could happen to you and the dreams formulate utilising all your inner fears and sometimes you try so hard to run away from that scenario that you come full circle.

I have always felt irrelevant and have played out my life in ways to try and make myself relevant. That just showed me as in control and with aim, therefore not in need of any help.

My toolbox – my coping mechanisms. They broke, I broke. I was lost. Unwanted thoughts that were taking hold 'if it could all end tomorrow the pain would stop'.

Life has felt like a battle to maintain an acceptable level of sanity, coping mechanisms to keep going and protect myself.

My chronic need for independence and being seen as strong/independent is ingrained by not wanting to rely or feeling like I can rely on anyone to be there for me. Again, fear to be let down. A lot of the decisions I've made that seem wrong or bizarre to others have been made due to fear.

Fear of being believed, prioritised, not being worth it. To be fair, this has also equipped me with an interesting and often very beneficial sense of humour!

Realistically, I probably had undiagnosed post-natal depression. I was so pig-headed about being in control and not supposedly struggling, or needing to rely on people that I over compensated by knocking everything I did out of the park. Mind over matter, I guess. It was like I needed to prove to myself that I was fine by succeeding at as much as possible. But it doesn't just go away, it always comes out in some way or another. And yet in trying to convince myself that I was smashing the whole parenting/juggling malarkey, I alienated myself. "How does she do it?" ended up being "it's annoying." I made myself un-relatable and alienated myself. Screaming in the far corner of my local Sainsbury's car park was not the answer. I was incredibly lonely and angry with myself and my choices and felt scarily unsupported. Trapped. But I needed to keep up the façade as I had a feeling I wouldn't have the option to be weak (as I saw it). I knew my husband was cheating or at least had cheated on me during my pregnancy with J. I knew that I wasn't going to realistically get past him leaving me to face a worrying pregnancy virtually on my own. The look on the doctors and nurses faces when he didn't even rock up for an amniocentesis when we had been warned it could start premature labour was humiliating. The same with my own health issues prior to the pregnancy, on my own (cue sad doctor's faces again).

I didn't have a choice, so it seemed. I kept busy as a distraction. However, the longer the procrastination, the bigger the fall. Living a lie has serious consequences.

20 weeks is not about 'woe is me'. It's about the 20 weeks of counselling I went through to understand what happened, patterns in my life, faults within myself and forging a positive and informed way forward. It didn't stop after 20 weeks, but it did give me the tools to keep on being introspective, to learn and help me through various old and new quandaries in my life. Come to terms with past mistakes and try to understand what I do and don't deserve.

We develop as human beings dependant on how we are nurtured. Yes nature plays its part and many of our traits, intelligence, illnesses and features can be inherited to some degree. But our confidence is gleaned from our successes, how we are received and treated. Our survival skills (and defence mechanisms) are developed through necessity whether real or perceived. We are not born untrusting and bitter, or fearful and sad. Nor are we born with fierce confidence to succeed and take on all that life throws at us.

But we all experience life differently.

I feel like some of what should have been better days have been stolen from me by thoughts, regrets and sadness some imposed by me, more imposed upon me. The anger that creates is just as damaging and all consuming. But you get buried deep among the dross, the deeper you get the harder it is to swim. Paradoxically, the deeper you are the less you function the way you would hope to, causing even further regrets, thoughts and sadness. In whatever form that takes. Not everyone gets a lifeline. The longer that happens, the less likely you are to see a way through. Drowning is so incredibly painful and scary that with little or no productive functioning, an end seems like a relief.

To those that may never have experienced these depths, it is unfathomable. I'm evidently one of those people that others come to for advice, coping methods and a semblance of common sense (I use this term quite loosely). Even at one of my lows I could still dish it out on request. And yet for myself, I just can't shake this feeling of irrelevance, despair and numbness. The way I would try and protect myself was to cut myself off from interacting with others. My lack of being myself just made me more paranoid that I was a hindrance to people's lives. Not being able to function properly meant I would say the wrong thing out of nervousness and slump me lower in embarrassment. My face was red raw and blotchy from stress and anxiety hormones. Drinking to 'cheer up' made me a fucking lush.

There is so much in life that to an outsider can be odd or even selfish. But only we truly know ourselves and our limits, self-preservation can be selfish, but it is also important.

This is a book about what a mess I've made, mistakes I've made and how not understanding ourselves can be incredibly damaging. I hope that my sharing will help you recognise what is needed within yourself to find peace and be the best you can be.

I've written this book at various stages of depression, sadness, happiness, sanity and surroundings affecting my mind-set. But that is life.

Paradoxically when you do try and work through these issues you want and try to forgive yourself and others, which makes you want to actually see things differently for your own mental health. This can actually cloud the way you write about the reality of a subject in particular when looking back, as it's healthier to let things go but then for this book, I was trying to write about something honestly and so I found it very hard to actually get writing sometimes as it would hinder my recovery.

The '20 weeks' concept developed and provided me with the tools to keep on learning. A conduit for self-realisation, perspective and to keep my introspective 'journey' going with all I still needed to process. It was more a way of highlighting what I needed to work on. This is it.

Chapter One
Week 1 – Where Do I Start?

Oh Jesus. I was sceptical and yet at the same time very willing to get help and 'guidance'. I was incredibly nervous about opening up, worried that I would crack up if one of the first questions was 'So, tell me about your childhood?' Hey, I know it's relevant, but is ball-achingly predictable and I thought nervous laughter would make me appear glib and not as 'depressed as I should be' to warrant this help. Luckily this question did not come up in the first week, and for that, I decided to give my councillor the benefit of the doubt.

Even more comfortingly, the second the conversation started, which was near enough along the lines of 'what has happened to you to bring you here'. I broke within seconds. Oh good, I'm fragile enough to not even front out the first question with good old Northern sarcasm and bluster. Nailed it. I have ticked the instability box.

Unfortunately, as much as breaking down quite quickly validates your predicament, it is not conducive to coherent explanations. Which also succinctly displayed my coping mechanisms of inappropriate humour being utilised to minimise my feelings and situation. Making light of an awkward conversation to not appear… too heavy. She's going to have a fucking field day with me.

However, I constantly found myself trying to show proof of what I was saying. Saying it out load sounded unbelievable. My councillor made it clear that 'proof' was not required, in fact despite my protestations, she wouldn't even look at what I had to back up what I was saying! I so strongly felt I needed to corroborate what I was explaining. Maybe that said more about what she was doing, she either didn't need it or intentionally didn't look to gain trust and take a position of the person she was to be on this journey. A safe trusted place/space. It was quite frustrating for me as I wanted to establish that this was not a subjective opinion on a series of events. Similarly, maybe she wanted to toughen up my lack of control over what people can know and understand.

We talked about who I was, what I do and what had put me at breaking point. My therapist listened and the Dictaphone recorded what she would later use to make sure she didn't miss anything that later needs to be brought up. We can't cover it all in an hour and even I was getting frustrated with the 'we may need to cover that bit in more detail another day'; 'this bit is part of a longer story'; 'it's funny when you look back on it now' – she did state that a few times, what I deemed as hilarious was needing further investigation!

Regardless, the first hour flew by. Tissues were used. The lack of a sofa for me to lay on was duly noted.

Chapter Two
Week 2 – Man-Thing

Quite often the catalyst for a downfall is just something that tipped you over the edge. The end of my relationship with one particular person was just that.

Ultimately, I was blind to what was, looking back, very worryingly obvious, but we can be blinded by love, a need to not be lost. Sometimes we just believe what we want to believe. He was a believable liar as he believed his own lies. He stated his perceptions as fact but he was not very perceptive. You cannot argue with a fool.

It started with his ex. We got together about 3 years after they had split up. We were all part of a wider group so its slightly dodgy ground on our part to start off with. They still shared a home but not a room. To cut a very long story short, it started off as an issue to do with an 'illness' where his ex wanted support despite being separated which is quite understandable. This morphed into needing to save money to renovate her flat so she could move in (I'm told 20k covered it) then she would move out and relinquish any claim on his property as it was his money that bought it and predominantly covered all expenses. During this time she wanted their separation being kept hush so as not to highlight her financial or medical issues to their friends. It was widely known but not confirmed. Then she actually rented her nicely renovated flat out to strangers and the alarm bells got louder so I gather, but any attempts to discuss it were met with tears and bluster. He left to work on a contract in another country with the understanding that that would give her the time to move out. When he arrived back many months later, she was there and arranging parties like she was celebrating her partner's return.

Then not surprisingly, the delay got her over the 7 year time-frame so she had a supposed more valid claim to the property.

His ex, – I was told that she ruins people and that to back down and obey/'concede' in regards to the image of herself that she wanted to portray I had no idea, how naive I was. So use to feigning strength that I was, I underestimated my own ignorant will. Let's be honest, I knew her myself and therefore I already was aware of her ways, but we all are unique. But a lot of my pig-headed belligerence was due to the supposed need to support an underdog, my ex was someone who had been controlled, bribed, tricked into sticking around, forced to be a part of a farce. Some of the bonkers tales I had been privy to seeing the 'proof' of which but let's be honest, in many situations we believe what we want to. Oh, the irony!

He used a doggy cam to watch his ex's movements during the process of getting her to move out of 'his house' so he knew when was safe to go home. She was supposedly violent and irrational so he wanted to feel safe for when he needed to go home. He put trackers on her devices, this was justified by him paying the bills on them. He always knew where she was so he knew when he could relax at home, he could access all her accounts, mainly Facebook and her email which he used to have a heads up of what she was doing in regards to their separation of assets through solicitors. Things he uncovered, which admittedly were shocking, but 100% private. They were used to fuel the justification, which I not only bought into, saw it as a need to defend the aforementioned underdog. Well, that definitely bit me in the bottom!

I had an acrimonious divorce but nothing in comparison to the relentless battle they went through, there were no kids or even a marriage to dissolve. It was horrific. Unbelievably slanderous, mudslinging that I was slowly but eventually a recipient of, threats, property damage, relentless legal essays, social bullying – the lot. It was so bonkers that it was hard for people not to be interested or involved. I remember him telling me that he'd bought a variety of website domains consisting of her name in different forms to upload everything about her to, the scams, bullying, vitriolic legal bumf etc.

I fell out with people too, based on believing his 'hard done by' rhetoric. His made-up world and lack of coherent perception. I honestly don't think I'll ever know exactly what did and didn't happen.

I have a pathological need to 'fix' people, more on this later. But he was like a lost puppy, drinking too much to avoid his home, a well-known fact amongst many of us and a childlike nature that was a cross between fun loving and craving something he didn't feel he'd ever had in regards to the 2.4 family. Ergo, great around my children.

He had developed issues dating back to when he was in boarding school from a very young age, not seeing his parents for many months at a time, staying with near strangers in the holidays or dropped off at an airport to travel with his younger brother to the Middle East to meet them for summer, stating that the main fear of this was not knowing if he would recognise his parents in arrivals. He developed a habit of rarely sleeping and just watching his dorm room mates throughout the time, a habit he was still partaking in when I was with him. He's never being able to articulate properly why. Spending many hours awake at the most dangerous times to engage in thinking, something that caused us many issues.

For some, I'm sure you can imagine, the boarding school option is great and for others is has created many issues of loneliness and abandonment that affects behaviour in later life. Both he and his ex had attending boarding school from young ages in common, but whether they operated on a mutual misery or could identify with issues they were experiencing only they can really say. It was an environment that he wanted out of and she clung onto for dear life reigning in on his insecurities.

*

To be honest, we all know that me starting a relationship with my soon-to-be ex-husband's friend in our social group was a contentious move. However, the vitriol I got in comparison to what had already been done to me to initiate the divorce made me dig my heels in. The move itself was shit but in comparison – I was a saint.

Honestly, it's partially my fault, we got together too soon after my husband, I was young, panicked and undoubtedly very messed up by the divorce. The signs were not that hidden, I guess I just wanted it to work and be ok. To prove that the issues caused that arose from us getting together we're worth it. Then there was the embarrassment of admitting that everything I had stood by him for could potentially be in vain.

Many people had come to me to tell me that he was a liar, 'not quite wired properly' was the term used frequently, but they were people who I thought had an agenda. My ex-husband unsurprisingly was one of those people! But cuddly fluffy man-thing who just wanted looking after, played Lego incessantly with the kids and couldn't pass a dog in the street without going in for a bear hug. How could that person be who they said he was?

But as the honeymoon period moved on I started to notice the absent mindedness and complete detachment from reality. Forgetting that we were actually out for dinner for my birthday or completely forgetting the day we were moving into our new place. I moved everything in on my own! Driving to a completely different town on a day out while on holiday to what we'd planned as a family because he'd imagined a different conversation during one of his 3 hour midnight awake stints. Hearing 3 different lies during a date night out about who did what to him, who owed him money and why. The obvious underlying thoughts in my head that all was not quite as I had initially though when we got together. How convenient his absent mindedness was when it suited him when challenged on this.

Everyone seemed to owe him money or had set him up which is why he was struggling financially, his business (of which there were 8–10) had taken a hit while dealing with his depression over how his ex had behaved. All this would rectify itself slowly, which I was told would in turn fix his insomnia issues and reliance on gambling to pay his bills. Especially when he would finally get his house back, sell it and we bought together. No more high rent. Life would eventually get better. This was incredibly believable as between us we had enough to buy with very little need for a mortgage. I was putting in faith (financially, as I was covering the lion's share of our living expenses) as an investment in our relationship – which as it turned out was all lies from him, intentional or not.

Every month was a battle of which lie I would get to explain why his share of the rent was late, I'd given him the wrong date, surely it was in there already, how much did I need again? The money wasn't the point. It was the dishonesty, the tiring rigmarole. The fact that he had so many businesses and virtually a mortgage free £800k property, he would always be first to the bar whenever we were out with friends, but this was a stumbling block.

I later realised once we did buy the house, one to renovate and make our own, that his credit cards were maxed out from being 'the generous bar guy'. Money for rent was harder to come by the excuses were a delaying tactic for when his gambling had not paid off in time for when I needed it!

This I did not uncover until we were well into our renovation, as we bought the house outright, I never really went through that process of finding out about what obtaining a mortgage inevitably would have uncovered.

When the money I was told we had left over after my contribution disappeared that is when it all imploded. Leading up to this point, the stress he must have been under of me finding out caused what I can only describe as a kind of stress induced schizophrenia or psychosis. Made worse that the counselling he had agreed to have when we discussed his depression issues following the fall out of his last relationship, was stopped to free up funds on the final straight to starting our new stress free life. Honestly, as I'm typing this I know how it probably sounds. Keeping up with the lies he told was not only impacting on him, but my response to it all was anger and fear. My trust in him was all but gone, I was scared and infuriated at which lie I would get next and had no faith in anything he said, which meant sex had long gone. My complete and utter disappointment and sadness made me look like a cold partner to our friends. Those that didn't know what was going on. Invariably I only confided in those who had kids and understood the related stresses of what was happening but weren't as close so as not to cause embarrassment on his part. Issues I now talk about in this book as any respect I had for him has long gone.

He ended up in the final hour explaining that we were £112k short even though we had only ended up doing half of the budgeted renovations and needed to get a bridging loan, these little gems come in at about 16% interest. A mortgage was off the table as he admitted he hadn't really earned in years. The bank of his mum and dad was exhausted from bailing him out of other issues. This would need to be paid off in a year, but ol' Delboy was convinced one of his businesses was on the verge of making a mint and quite frankly it was such a final hour that we had fuck all choice.

But then it happened. One night just after the kids had been picked up by their dad for the weekend, we were talking about our moving in date and he let slip that the kitchen would not have arrived by then and therefore most definitely not installed. Already generally in a state of irateness this was a shit situation and how could the kitchen people tell us so late in the day – how the fuck were we to deal with that with the kids, etc. He pointed out that he'd already told me the week before so I asked him to elaborate knowing full well this was a lie. First off he tried telling me we'd had the discussion at the very table we were sitting at and on which exact day. I pointed out that I was away the previous week in the Alps on a blogging trip so it was impossible and even when I got back his brother had come to stay with us for a few days and we'd been entertaining. This is not a regular occurrence, his brother lives in Perth, Australia, and had popped in for a few days on his way to doing an Ironman in Italy. His response was immediately that he hadn't, his brother had not stayed with us and had no idea what I was talking about. I just went cold and knew that this was beyond anything I could ever deal with. He was denying his brother had ever stayed with us.

A few days later he rescinded and admitted that his brother did stay but only for 1 night in his mind. But it was too late. I was now actually scared of him.

What followed was weeks of me repeatedly explaining that despite the horrible timing there was no way back. I was on antidepressants to help me cope with the constant stress, the anger I felt, fear of what I was living in. Essentially everything that I had thought him to be was a lie. It was impacting how I could look after my children and they were also uncomfortable with never knowing which side of him they were going to get. I spoke to him with his friends to help them help him understand, the same with his counsellor which he had then had to resume. I loved him and wanted him safe and understanding what was happening but this was way beyond something I could safely be in. But incredibly mindful that whatever issues he does have, the need for him wanting somewhere to belong was now in turmoil. We were a ready-made family for him, with a fluffy dog already included. It was like dealing with a child, his coherence of the breakup. Not in a derogatory way, tantrum way, more to do with simplistic emotional intelligence. Every day was a conversation about trying to help him understand. Each day was like ground-hog day.

We still needed to move into the new house as all our money was sunk into it, the rental home was now re-rented and we needed to finish as much of the house as possible to get it ready to sell. He took the big room that would have been ours, I took the small room and the kids shared the third.

He then did to me what his ex 'supposedly' did to him. It was transparent and psychotic. Simple lies and complicated truths. Great for the lazy. The truth should sometimes be guarded but it leaves inaccuracies of perception and understanding.

It came to a time where had to protect my own sanity and the safety of my children. I had to cut myself off from him, as much as possible. We split up in June and until we moved into the new house I was either on the sofa, or when the kids were at their dad's, literally anywhere else. I could not be alone with him.

He got to a stage where he started engineering scenarios to get a response from me or paint me as some sort of a bully to reign in on my guilt, he knew my empathic nature often conflicted me.

He even tried moving in a sofa that he had had in storage for years that he knew I hated because of my crippling fear of spiders. I did bring on an anxiety attack and beautifully in front of his friends.

Mission accomplished.

He ordered the real log burning fire instead of the agreed gas fire (that did look real) which he knew I wouldn't cope with, having outdoor logs in the living room. It was all to get a reaction.

There was a complete oblivion to right and wrong. He just didn't care. Reality and fantasy were all a blur to him. Just a few of the scenarios we had to endure, just to give you an insight of what I had to deal with while trying to protect my children and sanity:

Thursday 31st Aug – 9.39

He asked me to provide an email detailing his issues and incidents that have resulted in me needing to extricate myself from him for him to give to his therapist. He promised he wouldn't use it to harass me or yet again, bad mouth me to my friendship group. I provided the list and get numerous abusive emails in return. He later apologises for the abuse, but it's too late. The damage is done the things he responds with what he says to me and about me are disgusting.

8–9th September – 11pm to 1am

I went to pick up the dog from him at the clubhouse, he bought me a drink and asked me to stay, and kept on buying me drinks, and then an hour or so later he had a tantrum (he was drunk) and stormed out in front of Billy (Billy and his family rented his house of him when he finally got his ex out and started the process of trying to sell it). Billy said I shouldn't leave just yet, due to his outburst and then walked me home 20 mins later and made sure I got in ok. We were in the garden at the back of the house and he flew out, chased us and the dog out into the street and locked me out. 20–30 minutes later he came to the door in just his pants and let me back in but I had to squeeze past him. I ran to my room and closed the door, he opened my door and tried to blame me for the whole thing, he was very drunk and I told him that standing there in his pants shouting at me was unacceptable. He agreed to leave my room and went back to his room and proceeded to text me continuously.

15th Sept – 6pm to 10ish

The day before I'm due to spend the evening with my friends for one of their birthday's he gets drunk and harasses her on WhatsApp for 4hrs about what I have supposedly done to him, why didn't she support him and help us stay together then switched to how much he wants me back, then wants me to be supported by my friends, then on to how I'm supposedly robbing him blind.

27th Sept – 7.10am

Found his spreadsheet of where I was, day in day out. 60% of which were fictitious timelines of my whereabouts and interactions. He's been following me or just imagining he was. I got scared and got the kids out of the house before he woke up. We were gone by 8am.

12th October

Leaves me a packages with jewellery and a note. Totally bizarre and inappropriate considering what has been going on. He makes out that he wants the kids to give it to me to cheer me up using them as blackmail to accept it. I decline saying that I'm uncomfortable with it.

14th and 21st October

Both nights I stayed out and my Facebook was attempted to be hacked. The first one was after he drunk texted me at 1.30am telling me how sad he was when I didn't respond, Facebook was attempted to be hacked into within 20 mins. 21st I went away for the weekend and the same thing happened.

29th Oct – 1.30pm

Email sent to him to see if he would consider moving out due to how bad his lies, social bullying and the depths his depression/mental illness had sunk. Trying to sneak his new girlfriend in the house. It isn't healthy for all four of us, his drinking means he comes back at all hours and we never know when he will be there or if he will pull his weight with keeping the house 'viewing ready'. He responded with 'not a chance'. Then phones my best friend to have a go and swear profusely at her for supposedly 'passing on' information about what he had been saying about me. She hadn't told me anything but there clearly was something to tell.

Tuesday 14th Nov – 8.20am

Told him we had a viewing, could he not hang his clothes out in the kitchen. He got funny about not being informed, they never call him as I'm the one always in the house and in charge of the dog, they call so often and change viewings that I don't always have time to relay this to him. He got grumpy and insulting of my supposed attitude to him and his usual scary/oblivious manner resulted in me getting scared and asking him to leave, he walked out of the door then tried to come back in to shout at me, yelling 'why do I treat him this way', accused me of trapping his foot in the door and shouted at me to fuck off in front of the kids.

He called my friends to relay the usual dribble which made them send me a nasty text. Yet again making out I've involved them, I never mention my friends due to his previous harassment of them. His weird and fictitious texts followed.

Sunday 19th Nov – 11.45

Staring at me in the street as I was working home from my boyfriends, he just continued to stare as I approached, I crossed the road and he mumbled behind me that he's locked himself out. No call or text to say he was locked out, he'd just waited outside for god knows how long.

YOU DON'T REALISE HOW MESSED UP SOMEONE'S TREATMENT OF YOU WAS, UNTIL YOU TRY EXPLAINING IT TO OTHERS.E S

I chose to believe he was ill rather than evil. Who sets out to lie, destroy friendships and incite hate? I was becoming ill, a complete nervous wreck. It was affecting my ability to be the parent my children deserved. I was prescribed beta blockers just to be anywhere near him. Yet, I was made out to be the issue. They say you should not judge someone by their mental illness, but if they get others to judge you based on how you protect yourself from the repercussions of that illness – your respect for their privacy becomes harder to maintain. His narrative and actions were reckless. A man scorned. More on this in the friendship group section.

Unfortunately we still living in a world where women are easy pickings for being judged, not believed and insipid jealousy. It is the way of the world.

I got it wrong, how I let the break up play out. Oh so balls out wrong.

Chapter Three
Week 3 – The Breakdown

Written at 3am on yet another sleepless night, September 2018.

It is no longer any semblance of paranoia. I am actually hated. People love to hate me. I exude something that just makes people want to have a go and believe the most hideous of things. There is rarely an in-between, I'm even loved and appreciated or fucking despised. Better than 'middle of the road', I guess!

It's me that needs to change, I get that. But I don't know what it is that needs to change as the things people hate me for are based on lies. So I guess one of the changes needs to be to extricate myself from my friends and certain situations. I'm loathed to start again but I see no other way without being constantly ostracised. I no longer have the strength to pretend I'm ok.

Life is getting too hard. I won't constantly defend myself and therefore there is nothing I can do. I cannot sustain this, I cannot cope with being this reviled.

All my trust has gone. I'm lost.

*

The pressure just got too much. To be ok, to seemingly take things in my stride so as not to chance not being 'ok' and people not being ok with that. To be glib, to hide the disappointment or embarrassment of what others have witnessed. It made me look bulletproof, ergo not needing support or anyone. How could I need anyone? I've never experienced that.

My levels of OCD were horrific which made me too anxious a person to be around. I had control over nothing, not even my feelings, sanity, where I lived or my future.

The body and its central nervous system is complex. There is only so much we can overload our capabilities with and the result is malfunction and yet cleverly warning us that there is something very wrong. One of the features of my breakdown were ocular migraines which in short are like when I huge flash goes off directly in your eye and you lose sight for 20 seconds or so, imagine it for 30–90 minutes. Often with an internal ringing sound. You can't see, the fear is debilitating and you have no idea when your vision is coming back, it also can take away the focus of your other senses while trying to gage what the hell is happening. My body was failing me. It was very scary.

Never before had I fully understood why people wanted to hurt themselves or worse... I never thought I would understand this concept. I remember watching that scene in Love Actually and thinking the mother was selfish and self-absorbed. I'm sure many of us did before we all became more mindful and knowledgeable of the horrors people can endure mentally to put them in such a state that taking their own life is the only option they can envision. I am lucky that although the thought of feeling what I was going through was unbearable and I genuinely had no comprehension of an end in sight. The only sure way would be suicide. I did not want that. I dreamed of it all going away but I did not want that. I did however understand the want to inflict pain on yourself. When you feel empty, and numb, it's a way of feeling something.

It's a distraction. To feel something, anything different. To have control over what you are feeling instead of the overwhelming clusterfuck that was invading your sanity and happiness. Getting so close to understanding why people may choose to end their life, is scary.

What often goes hand in hand with many mental well-being issues is chronic insomnia. 3am is the worst time to think about anything emotional and is most definitely not conducive to getting back to sleep. Lack of sleep results in irritability, lack of productivity, mistakes, and the inability to think straight with furthermore endless other issues.

Over 9 months of little to no sleep. Which spiralled so many areas of my life out of control. Tears, brain fog, anger, short temper, lack of judgement. I look back now and just cringe! But obviously it wasn't funny.

The brain can only cope with so much. These overwhelming issues impacted my ability to function properly. What I really struggled with was my short term memory, something I still struggle with now. Being a parent screws with your brain anyway, lack of sleep more so, add in antidepressants and all of the above and maintaining any thought is an achievement. I'm one of those people that still remembers all the phone numbers of family and friends as a kid, can look at a set off instructions once and I'm golden. My trick when I was a waitress was remembering a table of 15's

3 course orders (with alterations), you name it. I was on it like a car bonnet – it sounds like I'm bragging of which I am a bit, it was a neat trick that got me some cracking tips. But then I turned into someone who couldn't remember if I'd brushed my teeth 20 mins earlier, if I didn't write a message or thought down within 10 seconds it would be gone. Only to arrive back at approximately 4.23am the next day.

'In regards to what was happening, I've never thought that what I'm feeling or what is happening to me is anyone else's business and yet I still wanted them to care,' I think.

I was scared, shocked at the situation I had found myself in, sad, embarrassed and paradoxically, the friends I did have left I didn't want to scare them off with my earth shattering sadness.

Chapter Four
Week 4 – Marriage / Divorce

We got together when I was 23 and a bit of a party girl, he was similar. Both a bit gobby and in a good/exciting stage in our careers. Regulars at 'the pub' where most people met and always first to the bar for shots. A date was quickly arranged and true to form with me it was a tad bonkers, my mum was randomly in town for the day and so I met her and a family friend for a quick catch up at The OXO Tower an hour before I'd arranged to meet soon to be hubs. There was of course a crossover and he met me mum on the first date. In for a penny in for a pound as they say! Tequilas next.

Needless to say I was smashed and unable to figure out in the taxi home which was my friend's house that I was staying at for 2 weeks between rentals. Honest. So we went back to his and I have no idea whether we drank more before we passed out, but that is all we were capable of. A relief when I woke the next day and saw the packed boxes showing evidence of his ex who was still to collect from their apparently recent break-up. I asked him to give me a shout when the process was complete but not until. Months later we bumped into each other and the rest is history.

The relationship moved quite quickly, we were having great fun and spending a lot of time together. Maybe too much fun. It was muted that we should have kids, his career was thriving and what an exciting next stage (!) which is a great decision to make during the honeymoon period. I'd been on the pill for over 6 years and assumed it would take a while, so while drunk on love and copious cocktails the pills were discarded and we jokingly half-heartedly bonked like no-one's business because we were convinced in the genius of our brilliant idea.

2 months later after a pretty spectacular night out with my buddy in Soho dancing the night away with drag queens and sneaking back to his rather rich sugar daddy's pad in Crystal Palace to drink more and watch gay porn on the projector while the SD was away. I crawled into work the next day in the previous days clothes, smashed a day's work out of me somehow. Only to get home to funding that my flat that I shared with 2 friends of mine (named The House of Thong after Toadfish in Neighbours had a similarly coined 'House of Trouser') had not only been robbed but ejaculated on. Talk about DNA evidence. None of us were too enamoured with staying there that night or removing said jizz, so when faced with such a dilemma you hit the pub. We all decamped to the pub across the road while the police did their work and we decided how to proceed.

I was at the bar waiting for to pick me up and whisk me away to an ejaculation free establishment that it dawned on me that I may be a tad 'late'. I quickly popped to Superdrug and when we got to his and I was freshening up before I joined him in the pub across the road from his house I took the pregnancy test, did the deed, chucked it in my bag and waited until I was glass in hand to look at the results.

The drink was not finished.

He was duly informed. I think that was the night he did a flaming Sambuca and forgot to blow the flame out before he stuck it to his stomach. The shot glass burn didn't go for weeks.

I still lived with my friends up until I was 6 months pregnant because not only did I love it there but also, nobody really knew I was pregnant. I was in shock and indeed conflicted, what happened to years of waiting for the pill to restore my reproductive cycle? I also didn't show until 5–6 months with a bit of clever dressing and it's surprising how ditching the booze worked well for my figure!

Eventually he made his case when arriving at my flat one morning to see a number of players from a particular professional rugby team asleep/making breakfast in our living room/kitchen, that it may be time for me to move in with him. *Sad Face.

My place up North had been sold to enable me to buy a property here, a family home to live in. His was going through the process too. The plan being that we would buy together until one day he asked me to sign a document stating that I would not be paying my fair share during maternity leave and therefore would I sign a document stating such. The alarm bells were ringing but I was lucky that I had my own funds due to buying my first property when I was 18, I had options. I had enough of a deposit to by on my own and was working, in those days the mortgage companies barely even checked your income if you had a decent enough deposit! I made sure he was well aware he was not required for me to get a house if he wanted to be a bit of a dick about it. It hadn't dawned on me that we wouldn't be in it together. I think he realised that I was not bluffing and 'changed his mind'.

We moved into our new home about 2 weeks before Leo was born, 2 weeks late I might add. There was a delay in the purchase (shock) and we had ended up pretty much camping at his friend's empty house for 3 weeks in the interim. It was shit and I'm a bit arachnophobic to say the least and this was a grotty bathroomed 'un-lived in' home. Needless to say I was at the gym a lot for showers and to use the toilet. Those who have experienced pregnancy will know the importance of a bathroom in the last few weeks/months and I was fucking petrified of using our toilet. I mean, spiders are a BIG deal for me. I didn't sit on my mum's sofa for 18 months after seeing a huge spider on it. My first ever trip to Australia involved me asking a stranger to help me use the toilet as I couldn't do it on my own in fear of red backs hiding in the rim. A lovely Brummie lady who luckily got it and saw the fear on my face happily obliged! A lot of my issues around tidiness stem from this fear.

Our new house was left in quite a state by the previous owners but all was unpacked before Leo arrived. Constantly cleaning, even on my first night out of hospital I was cleaning because I couldn't handle the dust. Most of which was done by me and his mum offered to help when she arrived following the birth. Because it was women's work and I was started to realise he was a tight arse. Believe it or not I'm not a huge fan of being a diva or asking much of people and was well known for just getting on with shit. Christ, I was in Starbucks getting a decent coffee out with Leo before he was even 24 hours old. But come on, would it have killed to pay for a cleaner, we were not exactly skint!

Singularly, this is not so much an issue. But there were many such incidents where if it didn't affect him it rarely was seen as an issue for him to deal with. Regardless of me and his son being a part of a team. He paid the majority of the bills and therefore he made the decisions unless I had the energy to make him think a purchase was his idea. My sole income was my maternity pay which did very little to give me any sway and went heavily towards me returning to work when Leo was 4–5 months, I needed that independence.

Your first baby and in fact having a child at any point is a very vulnerable state to be in. All my NCT friends were showered with flowers and new mum gifts. His paternity leave was used to host sporting events which meant me and my new born had to be shunted to our converted garage, resulting in my mid-wife questioning my safety and position in the household. I was embarrassed. He even left the hospital early after our second child was born so he could get last orders to celebrate becoming a father a second time around. We're talking about a 10pm birth! My current child-minder had our first born for an overnighter.

It was a standing joke that he did what he wanted and was more than happy to watch me hand-wash my car at 7 months pregnant while he chilled with a beer. The car was new and I loved it, but I'm a northerner and a valet was not something I was comfortable with (back then)!

When Leo was 18 months, I had a health scare. During one of Leo's visits to the nurse, she casually asked when my last smear was and on realising I had no idea, it was decided that now was as good a time as any. A few days later I got a call and was asked to come in, I insisted that such a request meant there was an issue and I'd prefer to know so I could panic less and if needed use my PMI (Private Medical Insurance) to speed up any process required. They were sure I had abnormal cells that had to be further investigated.

Within days, I was booked in at Cromwell Hospital with a specialist and very soon I had the diagnosis that I had precancerous cells and just how bad it was would be determined during the removal procedure. During my initial appointments and examinations I was told that my son should not really be attending these hospital appointments ideally and do I have anyone to help? I'm terrible at asking for help and the fact that he hadn't even offered caused me a mixture of sadness and embarrassment. I did manage to get him to look after Leo for the big op, which was a fucking relief as there were complications and I was not in a good way when it was done. I did my usual and lied that he was waiting for me outside in the car which was a requirement for me to not be released until I had help, when in fact, broken and sore I got on the Tube and he picked me up from a more convenient station nearer to home.

Of the many appointments I had, I think there was only one he attended which was the final consultation where it was explained to me that because of how much of my cervix they had removed due to the severity there was unfortunately a chance I would not be able to conceive again.

This was heart-breaking and in a pub a few days later I told a friend what had been going on and during our heart to heart, he stormed off as (and I quote) I was clearly paying him no attention.

I do keep myself to myself and have appeared strong but I do not take things in my stride, I struggle, I just don't tell anyone and I thought that they either wouldn't care or not want to be around me if I'm miserable or sad. I didn't want to be a burden. People don't support me at the best of times, in my opinion. But his attitude and involvement in something quite scary undoubtedly rocked us.

There was very little discussion of what the specialist had said, just that we would definitely want another one. A year later I finally fell pregnant, my sheer determination was great for our relationship! All went seemingly swimmingly until the 2nd scan when a large cyst on his brain was discovered. They did explain that they could sometimes disappear with time and they would need an amniocentesis nearer the end of my term to give a proper prognosis. I knew that my baby was active and responsive, never was there any discussion other than to attend the additional appointments at a specialist hospital near White City to keep a check on things and have the amnio when it was deemed safer to do so. The effects of the stress leading up to it and knowing I was on my own caused yet more issues and worries to be buried deep down.

When the time finally came around at 32 weeks, I was informed that the procedure can induce early labour but I was left to do the whole thing on my own. Even getting there and back. During the procedure, I cried all the way through, the doctors and nurses assumed it was fear and the related pain. It was loneliness and sadness.

At this point, we were engaged and work was more important to him than coming with me. My distance for the following few weeks as a result, I can only assume, explained why he started staying out more. Once until 3am with me frantically calling him every half hour. To this day I still haven't been told where he was. All I got the next day was the money in my account to buy a new gilet from Superdry that I had had my eye on. My/our son went full term and was perfectly fine.

However, we got married when my youngest was 3 months old in Barbados as he was determined to get the most out of his travel companion voucher and air miles. Most of my family could not attend as they couldn't afford it. His family could, just my mum and auntie came as well as a bunch of my friends who at that age had lots of disposable income! I'd hoped that when we were married any issues we did have would subside as there was a commitment from him that would assuage any further need to control me with finances or looking elsewhere. We already had our family formed and the situation was not ideal but not unfixable, in my opinion.

Our wedding took place 3 days after the skies opened up after the Icelandic ash cloud. There was a bit of a panic as to whether it would be able to go ahead. If ever there was a time that the universe was trying to send a message, I guess this was it!

*

He did love us and loved our kids but his priorities and ego often took precedence. In his mind, he was showing his love by working hard at his job. It didn't even enter his mind that things like booking our downstairs renovation, which involved interior and exterior walls being totalled, was a time when I may need help with the kids living in rubble. Instead we went to France for a week for the 'messy stuff' and I was to return while he went off to his usual 2 weeks FY kick off in the states. The kids were 3 years and 6 months old. Again, I was a standing joke as I just got on with it. It slowly grated on me that how I would cope was so irrelevant.

I regularly holidayed with the kids without him and either it was just us or with friends. Our holidays with him were decided upon by him with little input from me, unlike my trips without him!

Lots happens in a marriage and it's very rarely one sided. I've been rejected a lot of times in my youth. Disregarded in relationships, taken advantage of in friendships and my tolerance mistaken for 'being a walkover'. No wonder I like dogs so much! But this has contributed to how I behave/respond when I feel like a have been let down and it's not helpful. I shut down. Maybe it's all of this Prince saviour crap we were fed as children, the rom-com's that show an earth shattering realisation of wrong behaviour and the proceeding declaration of undying love, adoration and the willingness to work at and rekindle 'the spark'. If this realisation could happen at a stunning landmark, then even better.

However, because I predominantly live in the real world, this did not happen. What did happen is I got drunk a lot with my friends as a distraction. To help ease the loneliness of being in a soulless relationship and to feel alive. I was the sole carer of our children so hanging out with friends was mostly done in our home or with the help of my friends out and about. The joy of being the only one with children in our friendship group. The kids loved it, the attention they got and the extended family they got to experience.

*

A Self-fulfilling prophecy of dreams, and fears.

How we guard ourselves, and yet it can contribute to our 'undoing'. It's how we manifest our inner thoughts. For example, if you're so convinced your partner or friend will hurt you, you can 'protect' yourself so much that you disconnect or focus to much on the 'what ifs' and enjoy life less. Making you less of you and therefore you lose yourself, and so do others. Ergo, causing a search for more elsewhere.

One of my craziest and most occurring dreams was that I would have to contend with people in my own home taking the piss in some way and refusing to leave. Now I'm not too sure how much of a hand I had in this particular incident but still, here goes. After a night in with the kids before hubby had left the marital home and gone out for the evening, I went to bed after ironically watching a Desperate Housewives marathon and just as I was dropping off I heard the unmistakable sound of hushed 'slap and tickle' downstairs. I honestly didn't go down at first as I was in shock and I spent the next 10 minutes trying to mull over what was best. In the end, the sheer audacity and anger took over, as well as intrigue, so I grabbed my phone and went down. There through the glass living room doors was a bottle of Chablis next to the sofa, 2 glasses and one of my husband's friends from the local rugby clubs then girlfriend (married now I think) dry-humping him. Due to her frame it was hard to recognise her at first so I interrupted them, to ask for clarification. I did originally think it was someone else so he put me straight, "Hah, no it's…!" After replying 'oh wow',

46

out popped the camera and I got a good snap of them and pointed out that she should go home to *name (not providing it!) and I stepped back from the doorway to let her through. She actually refused. Hubs then came past the doorway to explain that she doesn't want to have to pass me and would I hide upstairs while she left. Even my dreams weren't this inventive. It's actually fucking hilarious in a way. Needless to say, no I did not move, not completely anyway as I did want her out of my home so I stepped aside a smidge further. She was smashed but she still managed to cancel me off her Facebook before she got to the end of our road.

Now this is the funny part and you do need to look for the humour in as many situations as you can. About a year later at a party with said rugby club after hubs was requested to leave our home (the photo came in handy – woohoo), the after party moved to mine. One does like to be the hostess with the mostest. Amongst the group of those wanting to come back was said woman, let's call her Enid to make it easier. To which she politely made her excuses and said she may just head back. I popped out for a fag as she was smoking too and pointed out that I'm happy for her to come, it's not my style to make people feel left out and to be fair, hubs just used you. She did come, with a whole crate of beer as a peace offering and her best friend who it turned out had also had a quick fumble a few months earlier with hubs around the back of the clubhouse. Honestly, you can't make this shit up.

*

The Divorce. I didn't want to break up the family no matter what, I was aware of the struggles, stigma and financial

47

worry being a single mum could bring. But it had got to a point where I was very sad and insecure. I would panic if I hadn't slept with him before one of his business trips, because obviously that would see him through! So much so that I was doing it perfunctorily and increasingly becoming angrier with myself. His attitude towards me was regularly commented on about him taking advantage or 'phoning it in' so to say.

I was so consumed with not being 'poor old Hazel' that I pretended I had it together. I needed to focus on what I could be in control of to keep me afloat. More drinking with friends while he was away, my house was the dinner house followed by copious amounts of wine. His idea of easing his conscience was always keeping the wine fridge stocked for me to entertain and have someone around for me and the boys. So long as his mum was happy to give him her M&S discount – he does love a bargain!

Even when the kids were ill, he was happy for his friends to pick up the slack while he was away, ironically considering how that developed. 'Keep her entertained'. I asked if we could start couples therapy to try and get across to him how this was a slippery slope. Try and learn new ways to get back on track. I knew I needed outside help to verbalise, steer and help us to get back on track. He did not want it. I can honesty not remember the reasons he gave but I'm sure it was along the lines of no time with a hint of the reality being the embarrassment of us needing it – 'we'll be fine'.

Then it finally happened months later. I saw a text that confirmed that who I thought he was seeing was thanking him for what was an amazing night together. I highly doubted it was that amazing. But all the same, it is one thing to end a relationship on a strong feeling of infidelity, but this was enough proof for me to think this was a way out without feeling too frivolous about potentially ended our family life on a hunch.

Within 2 days, I had seen a solicitor to understand my options and the process. One thing I knew was that I needed to fully know the score. He can be a slippery little fucker and I needed to know what I needed in place. This was September. By January, the divorce was in full swing once Christmas was out of the way.

I had sat him down and from what I gathered from our friends he was more than aware that the end was soon to be discussed. There was no mention of adultery as I knew this would anger him, embarrass him, ignite fear that I would go for the jugular and cause an unquantifiable response from him. I wanted out and a fight was obviously not the preferred route. I instead stated that there was clearly a breakdown, that I had repeatedly asked for marriage counselling to fix and as it never materialised, we were now at the point of no return.

We agreed to cite unreasonable behaviour against him as grounds for our divorce as a trade-off to what we knew was the case (albeit unsaid). I intimated without causing aggression that I knew that there were others. It was his preference and the easiest way for me to agree to what he deemed a lesser charge to get away without too much contention.

We discussed the next steps. Getting legal representation. Not telling the children until we arranged to make the spare room reasonable enough for one of us to move in to. Therefore keeping our news relatively unknown to our friends was imperative. We were not socialising together particularly anyway. Usual family outings would carry on for as long as it worked. I offered to take the spare room as it was nearer to the kid's rooms and his early mornings would wake them too easily due to the layout of the house. Very well thought out. Very cooperative.

The divorce started off with trepidation and yet high hopes that as he clearly didn't want to be in it, we could move forwards on the same page. It was all very polite at first.

Until it wasn't.

There were the various conversations about how financially this was the wrong time to split up in his opinion. Offers of a potential new and exciting life elsewhere (Sydney was mentioned), evidently still apart as at no point did he try to find a way to make it work, ask to try again, apologise or even properly discuss what was are undoing comprehensively.

We had implemented a routine of me going out one night a week (from memory it was Wednesdays) which was not hugely different to our current state of play, just more official, so that he was in charge of the kids and had his own proper time with them alone. Any and every other night he could and did do as he damn well pleased. We did have a nanny who as part of her contract did one night of babysitting every 2 weeks that was more often than not used and it was very rare that we attended the same pub. As you can imagine there were a few crossovers of venues, friends and a few bonkers nights out where I think others were more uncomfortable than we were.

Then there was Man-thing as mentioned above, who had throughout not been backwards in coming forwards with his 'behind closed doors' support. Declaring that he had already done the dirty on one of his old University mates and was tired of how he treated people. At the time I appreciated the information as confirmation of the route I was taking, I liked having an ally on the inside keeping me in the loop of what was actually going on. He was also fantastic with the kids when he popped by and really softened the blow for them. Unsurprisingly our regular chats did take a turn, the inevitable drinking really oiled the cogs and in no time we were discussing whether it was something that we needed to really consider taking forward.

*

The kids and I went back home to see my family for a few days arriving back on the Saturday. As mentioned above, part of the agreement with our nanny involved 1 night every 2 weeks of babysitting (or something vaguely close agreed upon each week) and as I had been away she had not done enough hours as per her salary so it was decided that we would utilise her for Saturday night as there was a party on at the local rugby club. God forbid hubs didn't get his money worth after not even seeing his kids all week! When it came to who went back to let her go at 11pm, all hell broke loose. Like never before. There is always that point in a divorce where the fake niceties wear off and true feeling start to pour out. I assume most of these times involve alcohol which makes everything so much better, obviously. It went something like this:

Me: Right who's going back to let [the nanny] go? Can I stay as it's been pretty full on this week?

Him: Nope, I'm staying

(It was one of those nights where the party was a great vibe, everyone having fun, hence us both wanting to stay on)

Me: Yeah but to be fair, it is your turn.

Him: You want to have the kids so much, go look after them or I'll go for custody and pay a full time nanny to do what you do.

Me: What the actual fuck?

Him: It would be cheaper, in fact I will go home and don't expect to get in later.

Me: You're drunk. This is ridiculous.

Him: I've been speaking to my solicitor about it already, you won't get a fucking penny. Definitely not the house. (Venom and spittle accompanying said sentence – it was like something I had never seen before and made my blood run cold. Shock does not cover it.)

Me: I don't want the fucking house, but you are not taking the kids.

Him: Well, let's see who gets home first then.

At this point, he made for the door. Keeping in mind that he had been drinking a good few hours longer than me, due to when I had got back with the kids so I was a tad more sober and quicker. I saw red and knocked him over so I could get past him and out of the door. I'm certain a C-word or T-word was used – from me that is. I ran like the clappers and got home which to be fair was only an 800m journey at best. But I got back in time, ushered the nanny out of the door so she wouldn't witness anything messed up and locked the door. My friend called to ask what was happening and why he was running after me so I knew he was definitely on his way. So I called the police. I didn't want anything scary happening in the house with the children there.

The police arrived within minutes either just before or just after him. They came in to find out what had happened while another officer stayed outside trying to calm him down. They assured me that many split-ups can result in a random argument that gets out of hand and would go and speak to him. Within minutes, they came back and confirmed that indeed he was sticking to what he had said in the clubhouse and was not calming down. Due to his temperament towards me outside they had told him that they were requesting he stay away from the property until he had sobered up and calmed down (requesting as his name is on the deeds and therefore cannot stop him officially until if/he is needed to be arrested). They suggested I got a friend to stay over to help in case he came back. My friend called her boyfriend and they both stayed until hubs arrived back the next day and assured them that I was safe. The police also told me to get a good lawyer that focuses on custody and getting my ducks in a row as he looked quite like he meant business with the animosity that was pouring out of him – to prepare for a fight.

So I did.

That is when it well and truly kicked off.

Lies about me abandoning my children and not knowing where I was most of the time – throw enough mud and some of it will stick. It was obvious as to who it had come from and why, he had form to play dirty, it was relayed to me by our at the time mutual friend. Yet, nobody cared about the lies.

Ironically, the only times I did leave the family home to get away, I took the children with me. Normally after either a dirty trick with money from him, something he had done to me socially or when my solicitor had recommended it due to his attitude during proceedings on a particular day. He did not take being caught out or losing very well.

There was the time he drained the joint bank account. We had one of those One Account's where all the money was in various pots and it all counted towards what interest we paid on our mortgage that was also included. I logged in one day to see that he had stolen £120,000 and transferred it somewhere that even to this day we were not privy to! However, after a quick call with my solicitor who promptly called his, he was told in no uncertain terms that this was not allowed and if it was not returned by the end of the day, his assets would be frozen. This in his eyes was a slap in the face and from what I gather was very angry that he couldn't get away with doing what he wanted with 'his money' and not initially compliant. This was one of those days I was advised to find somewhere else to stay until he calmed down. I stayed with my auntie a couple of miles away until he actually confirmed that he was understanding what he had done and how him choosing to remain in the family home required a certain level of behaviour.

There was the time that he tried to make out during the proceedings that I had an affair with his friend as a dig, when although it was not a great move on my part, it most definitely happened after our separation and way after he played hide the sausage with 'CG' (I won't use her real name as she was more than likely used to pad his ego and I have no idea if she really knows what she was a part of), however in my solicitor's response her full name and dates were used. This brought home to him just how much I really did know and for how long. His crappy and bogus diatribe was well and truly blown out of the water and it stung. He was told to keep the lies and games to a minimum unless he wanted his wife to provide yet further details, it was also pointlessly costly. That night the kids and I decamped to a friend's house, dressed up as a fun night of movies and popcorn with their favourite adult friends.

*

It was ok for him to cheat, embarrass, abandon and marginalise me with money, but when I asked for a divorce when I actually had all out proof of an affair, I was a money grabber. Then I started dating a friend of his, he was the injured saint.

Calling it a contentious move is seriously underplaying it. Our mutual friend, the kids 'favourite adult', the guy who clearly told me about my soon to be ex-husband's misdemeanours and kept me in the loop of what was happening behind my back. I mean...It's got EastEnders written all over it, yet with a more Suranne Jones, Donald Trump vibe.

There were many opinions about how I just didn't make life easy for myself. But a mixture of fear, finding comfort in an ally, lessening the blow for my children and genuinely feeling like I was in love after quite frankly a horrifically dispiriting relationship spurred me forward. The fact that it was quite well known that 'the friend' has always been more visibly available for our children was not lost on anyone. Apart from my soon to be ex-husband's parents who were blind to his priorities and shenanigans or so you would think. He is the apple of their eye, even witnessing him coming home at 6.30am straight from a party, balls out drunk and immediately getting in his Porsche to drive to his boat 10 miles away to 'sleep it off' was brushed off.

Do not get me wrong, regardless of whether you are a saint or not, knowing your kids have a new seemingly potential father or mother figure in their life hurts. But hand on heart I was definitely more mindful of this than I should have been, as I got crap thrown at me regardless. So many lies told to insight hate. Bullying encouraged. Emotional abuse through his financial and legal antics. The food shop credit card cancelled (even when he was still living with us!) just to cause chaos and feelings of entrapment and yet control on his part. Fortunately, I got an emergency loan to rectify this in the short term and get an order through the courts for a set monthly sum to be put into my bank account until an official maintenance agreement could be agreed upon. This angered him as it ultimately meant he was paying more and was not in control of what I had and when. He then tried every other trick in the book to make life unpleasant and created a few of his own. Most of which were recorded, proved and ultimately used against him legally due to the nature of what he did. As his anger and responses exacerbated, so did my arsenal. This all contributed to the court system not playing in his favour. Great in some ways but his only remaining option to make my life hell was publicly.

The threat of 'going for custody' meant that as much as possible I would stay in with the kids and not be seen to be leaving him with them while supposedly 'gallivanting'. Part of our agreement meant that he would pick them up on a Wednesday night to spend time with them so that I had a day of not rushing back from work. This was predominantly my night 'out out' or a mini night out when the nanny did her 4 hours contracted babysitting where we were both out. It was just a given that most of my friends would come to my house to socialise to make life easier for me. This did mean that he was out most nights spreading the word such as the aforementioned (and ironic) abandonment of my children, how I was bleeding him dry of money (everyone likes a money grabber), most of the lies were actually based on what he was doing when he was getting lazy with his originality.

Even proclaiming that we need separate parents evening appointments, as clearly his ego and agenda where more important than the already in short supply teacher's time! Standard. But as a favour they did this as a one off, for him to not only not bother turn up but to go to the local pub quiz instead to carry on with his social domination. But I try to look at the positive of as much as I can, at least this meant that I didn't have to suffer the intentional indignity of requesting it again. He tried claiming his flight from somewhere was delayed and so I sent a screen shot of him at said pub quiz on someone else's Facebook approx. 20 mins before his allotted time. Done and done.

I remember a friend of his actually checking in on me because, you know, "We know how he can be." Did that urge them to stop him or anyone else? No. Because people just let it happen. We need to stand up and be counted.

When you fall out of favour with him, he's is ruthless. Family, work, friends or anyone. And if he didn't like a waiter/waitress in a restaurant it was rare I would then eat my food in case my plate had received their revenge!

What is the commonality? White middle class men who on the surface are deemed presentable. Are they persecuted? Are they hell! Made accountable? Fuck no. Allowed to carry on regardless so people are not to appear as 'trouble', you know, one of those people? Give me strength.

10 Things I learnt from getting divorced

1. You can't stop people talking trash about you…
2. Sometimes I let people take advantage of me, just to see if they will.
3. People get scared that it's contagious. You know, splitting up.
4. You will discover strength you never thought you had.
5. That a 'rebound' relationship is a real thing.
6. That a low level alcohol dependency may be required at times of adjustment.
7. That Facebook is ridiculous, contrived and a weapon of mass destruction, paranoia and passive aggression.
8. That you will be forced to re-evaluate your life way beyond what non divorcees may require, but the necessity will hit you like a thunderbolt and possibly for years down the line.
9. You will have a friend clear out.
10. You develop an intolerance streak.

Chapter Five
Week 5 – The Group

But luckily when things like this happen, your friends have your back.

Firstly, let me state that I do know that I was dealing with some rather crazy situations that can be hard to get your head around in such stressful times that many of us live in anyway. We must protect our own sanity and head space. Not all ex-husbands go for the jugular, or have boyfriends who have serious conditions resulting in not being able to decipher reality from their stress induced psychosis. Nor am I a shrinking violet that to some I appear overwhelmingly strong. Sometimes you have to put up a stone front as crumbling is not an option. Or at least you think you have to. This can be detrimental to how people can or will be there for you.

Loneliness makes us vulnerable. I was scared to lose the friendships I had, until I realised what it was I was losing. "Don't be that friend who is needy."

Though what happened with 'the group' was unbelievable. During my breakup with 'Man Thing' I was petrified of the effect the relationship was already having on my mental well-being and my ability to be there for my kids while it happened. I was exhausted, angry, humiliated and financially I was in for a rough ride. But considering what I had gone through to be in the relationship and the responsibility I had to appear as a 'sane mother' to my contentious ex-husband put me in quite a pickle. Battle down, put up a front and ride it out. Don't let the 'haters' know they had won.

But let's be honest, mind over matter can work wonders. Keep telling yourself you're surviving and you can almost convince yourself.

I'd spent years dealing with his stressful ex relationship, business fails, financial issues and stress related psychological episodes. This had made me a nervous wreck and I was angry that it had!

When asked by my friends what had happened with the relationship in the first few weeks of splitting up, I had been blasé and evasive, citing that his lies, financial anomalies, lack of understanding for any issues with reality conception just got too much. And left it there. I shut down.

This did not give the required salacious gossip. I wrongly assumed that it was understood that I was trying to hold it together for my children and at least the real friends would not succumb to bull shit. The same bull shit I may add that I bought in to when I initially got together with him.

I was so wrong. What unfolded was beyond any imagining.

What did happen was he called on all of my friends, best friends who as a part of being in a relationship with me for the past 3–4 years had given him access too. Friends that I had been close to for 19 years, and in some cases a measly 10 years+ etc. Friends I had looked after, saw multiple times a week, cooked for, picked up when they were down, invited them to share my family life and anything they needed.

He turned up on their door (often uninvited) with his hangdog expression, lack of ability to decipher the truth and 'woe is me', relaying stories of how I'd just checked out with no prior warning (!) and left him heart broken and lost.

What I didn't expect was for them to take it as gospel, run with it and start what I guess can only be described as a desertion. Me and the kids were out and he was in. He provided a rhetoric that suited them, helped them avoid and forget other issues prevailing in the group. It was like they all had a saviour complex.

Within weeks of his first visit, I was kicked off a group holiday, excluded from a prominent birthday party (he was subsequently added and then given a bigger audience for his diatribe) – even events the kids normally went to, all n3 of us were all out.

On the rare occasion that I was given to ask why they were behaving like this, I was told that 'the group' were appalled with my behaviour. I pointed out the ridiculous obviousness of his lies that we're clearly insane ramblings of a very damaged man.

"I was stonewalling him," I'd repeatedly explained what was happening and why he couldn't undo what he had done. But he unfathomably just forget each time. So we had to resort to emails.

"I was trying to steal the house from him" A very expensive house that we had both bought with him owning a 2/3 share. I had struggled to pay what I had and was definitely not capable of buying the rest or legally being able to 'steal' it from him.

"He offered me £20k to move out for the house as a goodwill gesture." Yes he did however, the £20k was imaginary and our house was a 3 bed house that had all my money sunk into it. It needed to be finished ASAP and sold to enable me and my children to get away from him. With all my money sunk in to the house and only being self-employed, even with a fictional £20k I would still have not been able to rent a property even vaguely where we lived as I would need to pay the year upfront without proof of income. I also needed to stay in the area for at least 2 months to get my son into his chosen High School. Regardless, he was the one that caused the breakup, he was a single person who had been offered 2 different properties to live in for free where as I was a family of 3 with a cat and dog!

"She's cheating on me." He created a dossier of my movement over a 1 month period approximately 6 weeks after the split. Regardless of how creepy this was, it was also predominantly made up. Nobody appeared to have an issue with how incredibly scarily wrong this was.

I did regrettably and rather predictably start seeing someone pretty soon as I was constantly needing to be out of the house and it just kind of happened. Someone I had been friends with for over 10 years who unsurprisingly was also connected to the group (lazy dating, I know). That was by the by, I was even more so of a pariah, funnily enough the guy I started a relationship with, wasn't.

"She's making me sleep in a shed with a hose to clean with while she lives in luxury." He chose to stay in the garden room (with heating and built in sauna) of our £1.6 million property during a major construction couple of weeks even though he was offered a 3 bed house to stay in while his friend was abroad. A friend of mine lent me and the kids her 2 bed tiny cottage while she was visiting her mum in Spain as the property wasn't safe for the kids. But that's a boringly practical story.

"She constantly verbally abusive" Poor him. No, but I am a northerner who loves a swear word. When he came home drunk and left the oven on for 6 hours with pizza in it while the kids and I were in the house, yes I was pretty pissed off. Same with spending a few hours with a friend in the kitchen while he sat in the living room in the dark staring at us. He is quite a large rugby bloke and the friend I was with does not scare easily but she has refused to ever speak to him since. We did take picture as proof as it was just so unbelievable. That inspired a few choice words predominantly through shock, fear and embarrassment.

I must point out that I got to a stage where I documented everything I could as proof, as even I struggled to believe myself at times.

There was only 4 people whose opinion I really cared about and didn't want to lose. One of which was a warrior who held her ground as long as she could, but ultimately she was in the pockets of the more dangerous ones, constantly at the events were trouble was caused and I could see that it was affecting her mental health being pulled in so many directions. Whenever she saw my broken state I could see it destroying her self-worth (not over egging it, she is/was quite a conscientious and sensitive person). The more I broke, the more it crushed me to see her happy and smiling with my ex who was causing me so much pain. It eventually took its toll and we parted ways, hopefully temporarily until life was easier/clearer, but unfortunately different path was formed.

Then there was the supposed 'loveable drunk' of the group that regardless of how infuriatingly embarrassing his drunken states constantly were you couldn't help but weirdly find it endearing. We did a lot together throughout our 10 year friendship from sharing Christmas's together, cooking for him multiple times a week, incorporating him in my family as he had not the best one himself, propping each other up constantly and just doing and being what friends are. But I wasn't even given the opportunity to ask why he suddenly rejected me and the kids. Keeping in mind that I was not to know what nonsense was being peddled.

Anyone outside the group, who may I add were brilliant and not so impressionable/gullible, attribute his behaviour to many things, me turning him down and never showing interest in him that way was the favourite. Not a stance I shared. A drunken misogynistic dick was the most common reasoning.

Then there was my best friend and her partner. A friend of 19 years who, let's be honest we knew of each other where all the bodies were buried. You name the scandal, we'd probably experienced it. Each other's wingman, support network, 'partner in crime' (not always literally), the one we turned to when to others what we had done or needed was off limits. When we split from our boyfriends, we knew what each other needed, whether it was saying what was needed to save the relationship, or getting off our heads because it was happening either way.

Her partner of 10 years, but who I was at least vaguely friendly with for an additional 5. The one that came on the family holidays and played with my kids because their dad couldn't be arsed, took them to the pub to watch rugby, jumped in the pool on holiday to save one of them as FF was too engrossed in his phone. His confidante when struggling be that emotionally or relationship wise. We shared a love of hiding from people who got on our tits and developed quite an honest relationship if not at times I'm sure, much to my friend's annoyance. But as I'd frequently pointed out, it often worked in her favour when he was being grumpy or she had pushed him too far in their relationship.

He unequivocally ditched me. I found this out through my ex who pointed out that everyone hated me because of what he had told them. I adamantly defended that that indeed was utter bollocks and to just leave me alone. Until weeks later I found out it was true when the cold shoulder became more apparent. And being ditched from the friend's birthday dinner.

Shock doesn't cover it. Anger was definitely playing a part! When I eventually managed to get him to engage, only by WhatsApp may I add, what unfolded broke my heart. Evidently I didn't give him enough information about what happened so he had no choice but to hear the other side.

My friend was semi left in the middle to navigate how she would handle what I thought would be a relatively explainable fix. Then she was the spokesperson for ditching me from the holiday and used the excuse that the men were very adamant that I was to be left out and she was just the messenger. How very woke.

21 September 2017

Hey Hazel, clearly it's a bit awkward with the group and few people so what are your thoughts on the Costwalts? As it's ▓▓▓▓ birthday thing do you think it's best you don't go and I give you the dosh back? This whole situation is just horrible I hate it but guess it is what it and the other alternative is he doesn't go!!!
🙈😬😔 10:16

If that's what they want, fine. I think their attitude is atrocious but so be it. Yeah just refund me the dosh. Xx
10:57 ✓✓

It's a shit situation but they are so off about it all, the atmosphere is dreadful at the moment when we are all together. I know both ▓▓▓▓ and I want you to come but the others are of a differing opinion sadly. It would make for a crap w/e all round which really sucks 😔 xxx

You can't send messages to this group because you're no longer a participant.

||| ◯ ‹

I was not completely unsympathetic to how tricky it was but naïveté and oblivion was used to back up crappy/cruel behaviour and keep reiterating 'what I was doing' was making people uncomfortable. Very conveniently forgetting that 'what I was doing' was a false reality created by a very damaged man of which she had repeatedly witnessed his challenging view of reality, ability to tell the truth and even been the victim of his lies/social bullshit repeatedly. But that didn't suit the agenda.

Token visits were made to me before or after events going on only minutes away from me, where I had been ditched and my ex was slotted in.

When my ex created WhatsApp groups harassing her, her partner and myself – I was blamed for the intrusion and affect the stress was having on her pregnancy. The irony was incredible. It was all his doing.

This was a situation created by my ex, that was causing the unnecessary stress and not only that, took me away from my best friend who needed me during her pregnancy. Like I needed her throughout mine. The anger, unfairness, frustration and sadness of this compounded the breakdown that was already developing.

So I took a lot of it on the chin. Put my friend first, and tried let things just smooth over with time. But you teach people how to treat you. The bullying did not stop and I was constantly treated like some sort of gold digger. Being told to just 'tone myself down' to get people to like me. It was suggested I held a gathering where I let people ask me questions so I could put them straight. What the actual fuck! Like my mental health, children's lives, finances, fears and bra size was public property.

I couldn't believe this was happening to me. I spent half my time in shock at what was happening and the other half of the time in shock that the incredible bullshit was being supported. But then again, I bet there are many women reading this that are not terribly surprised.

Let's be honest, all the reasons for what people chose to believe what they did, was heavily embedded in misogyny, jealousy and narcissism.

There was however a lot of peer pressure from certain members of the group who were not happy with those that fought my corner.. I understand this, it's how bullies work and it's hard to risk going against them for fear that they turn in you and in some of the cases, this would not be their first rodeo of being on the receiving end.

You may think this all sounds toxic and why would I care? But when you're in it, it can be so all consuming. It was all consuming and any issues that I was having due to the stress of why I broke up with him suddenly just overtook.

To be cut off by what I had classed as family, certain members of the group I had no issue with losing, they weren't really a loss. But the others, it was like a mass bereavement, while being bullied, while being constantly scared in my own home and socially ridiculed.

I broke.

Eventually I sent the following to the 2 girls who were knee deep in the group that I had any (irregular) contact with. The second response being from my long time best friend who was also one half of the couple mentioned above in regards to who the kids and I did everything with.

*Hi ******

I've been agonising over what to say (if anything) to you both in regards to where I am right now. We all know it's all a bit crappy and awkward.

What happened to me over the last 18 months really knocked me for six. You'll never understand what it's like to be on the receiving end of someone like [man-thing's] crazy shit, what that can do to you when trying to protect your own sanity and your family, especially when being under the same roof. The pressure was immense. But to deal with that while friends and people who I saw as family repeatedly supporting him and those that decided that his crazy perceptions of reality was real... I've been shocked at what you were all so happy to not only believe, but not even question me about its accuracy. I've spent that last year or so being a cross between offended at the assumptions, your willingness to even be in the same room as him (and others) and yet conflicted with thinking I should never have had to explain anything.

Whatever tricky situation you found yourself in, and I'm aware of the perception he can give off and your close relationship with the 'protagonists'. I've tried to accept this. Life is not black and white. However, I did not deserve how you all collectively treated me. I can only assume it was something else I've done that I'm not privy to and I apologise for whatever I did to offend you or make you feel unhappy with me. I'm aware of my many flaws, none of us are perfect, but I'm working on them.

I got to a stage where I was questioning my own worth, so much so that my depression which both of you have been aware of has been something I had to prioritise. Ending things with [current partner] (after Man-thing) gave me the chance to really draw a line under that era of my life where, for whatever reason I was repeatedly humiliated, abandoned and people I thought were good friends and in some cases like family, had the audacity to believe his nonsense, support it and treat it like cheap gossip with no regard to the effects this would have on me and the boys. This crushed me. Even if half of his depictions of reality had been real, I still didn't deserve how I was treated by you all. What is done is done, but as you've pointed out (just before Christmas) you vehemently support their stance and have no issue with their actions in regards to some of these people that contributed greatly to the shit we went through with him.

What was happening to 'Man-thing' was not only between him and me, it was a very sensitive matter that we had been battling for the 6–12 months leading up to the end in June. It was also at a time when '****' was pregnant and not only did I want all my energy spent on keeping my kids safe and sane (and feign a sense of normality for them), I didn't want to put pressure on you at a highly sensitive time. It's a shame others didn't have the same sense of decency.

I've spent much of this year so far working very hard to get back to me again, I'm seeing a counsellor, gaining lots of downtime, trying to focus on the right things and stay away from situations that increase my anxiety or make me feel low.

Sorry for the long bastard email or if you find it tedious but it is important to me.

I hope that when I'm strong again you'll still want to be friends and also you know I adore (names of their children).
H xx
(3rd Feb 2019)

Response no.1:

Response no.2:

3 February 2019

Oh darling I've just read your message - you do what you need to do but when you are ready I'm always here to pick up as we left of and be friends. I can't say I'm not upset but all I want is for you to be ok and if that means having a break that's fine with me but just remember I'm always here and be happy to have you and your boys in our lives again. I love you xxx 17:10

Thanks xx 17:28

*

While this was happening, I found it helpful to write down what I would like to say, even though I knew I would not be given the chance to air it even if I should. When you write down what is plaguing your headspace, you can order your thoughts. Know that what you would like to be able to say is recorded somewhere so that your brain/psyche can be freed up. A bit like a brain dump. The following is just that:

Ultimately, how you treated me and what you helped that man, and others do to me and my children was abhorrent. Even if half of his lies were true, I nor my children deserved it. But as a group, you were cruel and misogynistic. I want no involvement with what you deem acceptable.

The deafening irony of you thinking my predicament is a burden, a predicament you contributed too blindly with your cowardice and jealousy inspired narrative.

I used to be strong, but you broke me. If this happened to anyone I knew, I would be petrified for them. Maybe you are scared and find comfort in your distance, your callous rhetoric. The lack of care you gave in supporting such hateful rhetoric, the lack of consideration for my mental well-being or the effects it would have on my children, children who you are indescribably close to. It was shocking, but overall heart wrenchingly disappointing.

The whole debacle was brutally unkind and spineless. I was punished for trying to keep my shit together throughout the worst time in my life.

When screen-'shotting' the various messages from my 'best friends', predominantly to write this book, I occasionally accidentally read a few of the words in them that sent me into an uncontrollable downer for days that I just couldn't shake. The words plagued me and the injustice of their lies and incomprehensible narrative. It would plague me for days/weeks, the fragility of your mental state after certain circumstances is then more susceptible to 'dips'.

It takes strength to walk away from toxic people, it's not always a weakness to not forgive. What is weak is tolerating bad behaviour because it's easier.

What hurts more than losing you is knowing you're not fighting to keep me.

What I should point out that a couple of years after this all kicked off I managed to reconnect with the only 2 that really mattered, the couple. What is meant to be, will be.

*

Ugly Face incident

So what do you so when you are losing control of what you thought was an upper hand in a situation? The truth was coming clearer in regards to what they had been a part of affecting their false sense of morality. Do you get on with your life or start more rumours to conjure up 'pack support'?

It got brought to my attention that the latest line was 'Her son called my girlfriend an Ugly Face'. From a 52 year old man in regards to his girlfriend, referring to my 12 year old. Granted I was told it was supposedly heard while they were very drunk, very well-known local drunks, and yet it's all about flinging enough mud isn't it. The accusation from the aforementioned 'loveable drunk' mentioned previously.

However, it turned out my then boyfriend knew he had done this and was spreading it wide, but not told me and was still socialising with him. Even briefly, I did too as (as a result of occasionally attending the same pub) I was unaware until quite a number of weeks later what had been said. Fuming doesn't quite cover it. It was hugely understood I gather, that it was nonsense and drunk ramblings that most people who knew my sun definitely knew wasn't true. But pack mentality forces people to sit comfortably on the side-lines for fear of being ousted or next on their list. That's how bullying works. Let's just reiterate. A 52 year old man is telling lies about a

12 year old boy, well known amongst the group as being ridiculously polite and fun, for social gain.

Now, let's just for arguments sake, take the position that he did say it. For what reason would they need to tell all and sundry? To intentionally humiliate his girlfriend. I despaired. People who actually know the nature of my oldest quite rightly thought it was baffling, ridiculous and out of character to say the least. But of course, it was supposed to be a slight on my character, not his. 'He's just using his mother's words', maybe? On the basis that that name has never crossed my mind and most definitely has never been said by me what person conjures up such a hurtful name against their girlfriend? Although it was undoubtedly based on my predilection of calling my ex hubs (along with many an ex-wife I'm sure) 'Fuck Face'. At least, it was catchy and beautifully succinct.

The intention is clear, but who makes something like that up about a 12 year old boy for social gain? Asked and answered.

Shame on them, their lack of interest in the truth and desire to jump on a bullying bandwagon. Mainly because of a misogynistic agenda and to distract each other from their own spiralling behaviour, predominantly towards each other. However, this sort of behaviour, when the reality and truth starts to resurface often results in a need to justify their behaviour. Resulting in a search for anything that could cast more shade.

SOMETIMES PEOPLE PRETEND YOU'RE A BAD PERSON SO THEY DON'T FEEL GUILTY ABOUT THE THINGS THEY DID TO YOU

A finale to end all

So sometimes when you're caught in a toxic situation, where all normality is questioned, deciphering who you are and what is ok can get muddled. A mixture of wanting to not leave a situation sourly or let those who wanted you out, through persecution, to win. Ridiculous right? We all want a happy ending, however, the one I got was not involving me. Well, I was part of it, just not consciously.

Just before the global pandemic, COVID-19, I managed to finally complete the purchase of my new property. A place bought solely by me, with only me on the deeds, perfect for me, the kids and the fluffies. Luckily we got it at a steal due to me not being in a chain and their previous buyer falling through. It was a quick deal and one of those things that you just feel is meant to be. There was little room for procrastination and various circumstances meant that I just cracked on with it on my own. It's the 4th place I've bought so I'm not new to the process, did not need my hand holding nor did the speed they wanted the sale to go through give time for my current boyfriend to offer his superior knowledge. Tongue and cheek meant however, he is a property developer and was quite 'put out' at my lack of needing his help. It was already fully developed though!

The place would give me the eagerly sought independence and security (both financially and my own 4 walls) I have been craving for years. Rent is a killer and you're less resistant to make a rental your home when each picture you put up is £50 off your security bond! The completion date was a big deal. I'm a single mum on a part time salary. Getting the keys would be an emotional day filled with relief and excitement for me and the boys.

I'd planned to pick the boys up from school and let them run around, just us and the dog before we (the boyfriend and I) cracked open the fizz and ordered a take away. Best made plans eh? The previous owners were late getting out and tidying up, not drastically so, I got into the place by 4pm instead of 1pm. I had a drink in the local while waiting and to be honest I was only an hour behind 'schedule' which was relayed to him. Half an hour into being in my new home, I called to see when he would be over. To be told he's not, he has made new plans, evidently he felt like the plans we made were too vague and not seemingly directly involving him. But, there was a party elsewhere so he was going to that instead and it was important. With 'that group', I was ditched to hang out with the local drunks who have given me hell. The importance of the evening was that it was someone's birthday (he'd evidently known about it for ages so could have told me), the person whose birthday it was he'd never met, nor was he even still alive and hadn't been for many years. It was just a flippant excuse to put me in my place or express his authority you may rightly assume!

Honestly, it was the final straw of his ego taking over. Myself being embarrassed in front of my kids as he'd ditched our plans, yet again. Me being upset at a time I should have been elated. Yet again I'd let that group affect something that was happening that I was really proud of. I was shocked and hurt, but evidently my friends had predicted it. This they knew would create issues with me being less dependent on him. And yet again I couldn't resist checking Facebook (why!) to see him having a curry at midnight with the one woman from that group who he's admitted fancies him, with others too, but predominantly all cosied up to this one woman who was giving him the attention and adoration he required. Ego is a bitch.

Needless to say we were finally over. Once the initial anger subsided we decided to remain friendly for companionship and our now blended families needing a less abrupt end. Nobody else was involved, we just make each other incredibly sad in a relationship but hopefully all the things we did like about each other could potentially remain. The occasional dinner, cocktails, dog walks and sounding out the crap going on with our families.

Then COVID-19 upped its game and quarantine was imposed. Mix in his chronic loneliness, my obsession with feeding people and our joint love of espresso martinis, it was decided that we should lock-down semi-together. Half the week at mine and half of him at his. Granted it was bending the rules slightly but his obsession with 3 showers a day worked in his favour.

Many weeks went by of living like a sexless couple, not dissimilar to how it was before, but at least now it was off the table and not a bone of contention. No pun intended. Yes there were a few drink fuelled emotional nights, nights with zoom quizzes (for the love of god) with his friends where they blatantly hadn't been told of our new status. The one drunken snog and yet repeated reminders of the pandemic creating a situation not conducive to the reality of where we are.

We often slept in the same bed when he stayed over, it's a big bed and I most definitely don't sleep naked, with an additional beagle barrier between us. His birthday was looming and the request for me to go to his to celebrate with his kids was procrastinated over as restrictions started to ease. Stepping in someone else's household during the arse end of strict lock-down was quite foreign. The assertions of woe is me and would I like help choosing him a present etc. was getting scarily like he thought we were falling back into a routine similar to when we were together. His stroppy attitude was creeping back in and the kids were getting remarkably less tolerant, but the idea of seeing his kids, which I adore – marred with my usual sarcasm, combined with my kids having a change of scene and hating to miss out on a party, it was set.

I was in the phase of repeatedly reinstating our predicament while not wanting to be a Debbie downer nearing his birthday.

I passed out one night in bed after, let's face it, a spectacular parmigiana and perfectly paired red wine. Netflix wasn't even switched on and put on timer as I put myself to bed, I was out, knackered. Dog in situ, probably the cat too but I can't be sure, she's sneaky. During the early hours I was suddenly but discreetly broken out of my sleep by a grunt and deposit of sperm on my back. I froze. What the fuck do I do? Have I just been spunked on? I kept my eyes closed and pretended to remain asleep. I still don't know whether that was right or wrong. I think I wanted to see how it played out, god knows. He got up and walked off to the bathroom mumbling something along the lines of either 'I know you're awake/liked it'. Came back with toilet roll and wiped me. He wiped his spunk off me. Then rolled over and went back to sleep. I however, did not. I didn't want to fall asleep and not know if it was just a nightmare. How the fuck had I just been ejaculated on by someone I've known for ages without being seemingly awake? How many fucking times has this happened? Am I to blame? What the actual fuck.

I decided to make good use of my insomnia and plan what to do next. I'm proactive if anything. So after 386 different ideas of how to lose my shit, I finally settled on saying in the morning that I can't believe how well I had slept and did he sleep well? Yes I played dumb to see if he said anything along the lines of 'you slept all night? Fuck me Hazel I thought you were awake in the night and I got frisky, I honestly thought you were a part of it. I may have taken things too far, I just thought you were sleepy'. Nope.

"Did you? Lucky you." That was all I got.

There was no acknowledgement. This surprised me more than I thought it would. The next few days were quite hazy and let's be honest, quite a few excuses were made to not see him, even though I knew the birthday was days away. Even after that, I didn't want to be a bitch. Paradoxically though, any friendly affection had drastically dwindled into ejaculation-esque oblivion. This would later be used against me. I shit you not dear reader.

The fact that he knew I wasn't comfortable with him touching me, makes it all the more sinister. The way he had behaved when we were together had dwindled much of our intimacy as is often the case when a relationship breaks down.

The birthday went well, due to being able to focus on his kids that I hadn't seen for months. Burying myself with cooking, cocktails and pretending I didn't know about what he had done. Only I knew. If I didn't tell anyone, I couldn't be judged for dealing with it this way. My urge to not end things, things being our 10 year friendship with a rapey vibe. But my hackles were up, I was like that kid avoiding the creepy uncle. Yet again, my supposed need to try and protect others was failing me monumentally. I really am a weird piece of work sometimes.

What is most disconcerting and upsetting about the whole event was how I felt trapped and too scared to tell anyone what had happened. 'The Group' would have either not cared or disbelieved me due to past tales spun out or their preconceived agenda of how irrelevant I was, or 'deserved what I got'. On the other hand, my group had frequently and relentlessly warned me about his involvement and behaviour towards me in regards to that group and how I was setting myself up for a fall. Unsurprisingly I always think I know better!

Either way, at a time when I was distraught, confused and feeling vulnerable and embarrassed I had no idea how to deal with the situation.

Then a few days later sitting with friends on the Green, after the previous day telling him I needed to cancel dinner plans because, well, you know why. But I said that I was feeling a bit down and under the weather. He walked straight past us, ignoring us completely, not even acknowledging us. Not a complete surprise as he was meeting 'the group' and separates it quite spectacularly. Still to ignore us was bizarre.

This not surprisingly sparked a few questions. Especially as his own daughter had only just left us and said she'd had a huge fight with him regarding him blaming her for stealing some wine that he'd a few days later admitted he had drank, forgotten he had and she was still fuming.

Due to the second gin and just being quite flabbergasted (I'm always happy-ish for the excuse the use this word), I explained what had been going on. It was a 'this may be a contributory factor' kind of conversation that I started quite meekly I'm ashamed to say. My rather appalled friend who is normally quite reserved in her judgement, pointed out that even if her husband did that it would ring divorce bells and surely that was enough to finally get me away from having anything to do with him and any connection to that group.

This caused an outpouring of grief for what someone I had seen as a friend had done and the subsequent behaviour from him just hurt, incredibly so. I went home, still in tears but just needing to process what had happened and how yet again, I just let people treat me this way. Whether they think I deserve it or not was no longer on my radar, I need to own this, speak my truth and (sorry) get closure.

I sent the following, with the obligatory quick approval from my good friends, Kate and Sally (who I had been with on the Green):

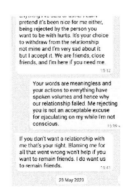

The response floored me. Do I need to take ownership of why he did this? FML, I'm out. Actually if I hadn't have got such an egocentric and misogynistic response, there might have still been some semblance of residual friendship feelings. See, positive attribution in action.

It's degrading, it's meant to be whether they are doing it consciously (how ironic!) or not. This is Male Egocentric assault and narcissism at its finest. This is not ok. Don't let someone gaslight you.

Misogynist Sympathisers – What a term, a term that is quite worrying and yet can be such a trap, an archaic mind-set that we need to work on. It relates to men and women who side with misogynists' views either through laziness, peer pressure, fear to stand out or to belittle those who threaten what they know and are used to. Fear and jealousy so closely overlap. There are also those that just crave to be seen as the conformist. Women that stand up for themselves or strive for independence are still perceived as being 'trouble makers', you know 'she's one of those'. That is not to say that if you don't stand out you don't have such attributes, they can come in all shapes and sizes and yes we are all different. Different goals, dreams, experiences and support networks. We also do not always have the freedom or are able to display such independent thought – I get that.

Ask yourself, have you been taking the easy route to be liked and accepted? Sometimes we are not aware of our own actions or the implications of such. Women be better. Men be better.

Chapter Six
Week 6 – Dad

I had quite an interesting relationship with my dad to say the least. I was definitely frowned upon for wanting and expecting more.

I didn't fit into line when it came to my dad. Everybody else were either having a different experience or were very accepting of what I felt was a situation where we should demand better. Yes I was the youngest one, but that wasn't enough to explain it.

I was the one that often refused as a child to go to see him on his allotted Sundays. Citing that he did very little with us other than drive around aimlessly, sit in a pub (ironic as I love that now!), I didn't like his partner and I was constantly berated for causing problems being a vegetarian. On the days that I did go nearing the age 12+, I had quite a few drama commitments which involved him needing to take me to my stage school rehearsals when shows I was a part of were approaching.

I really hated the Sundays that we were expected to visit his partner's family who lived in quite a rough area and were wildly racist. I was branded as awkward and moody.

I was annoyed that he wasn't better. I was ashamed that he let lazy attitudes make him seem like someone he wasn't. He was well travelled, funny and clever. But I was angry and held on to that anger (like the stubborn person I can be!) that he didn't be someone better than he was more than capable of being.

There was the time that his rather tacky, and unfortunately long term partner had a family event in their home and one of her nieces bought her new boyfriend who was Asian that she referred to as that 'P*** Bastard' in a room full of people to his face. I stood up and made it very clear that I longer wished to spend time at my dad's house with that woman. I understand that the man in question was probably and heartbreakingly very used to such attitudes but I couldn't sit in a room where this was just accepted, rather than cause a fuss.

It was rarely talked about, other than my dad asking me later 'what all that fuss was about'. I just stated that couldn't be on-board with her, she has repeatedly being quite toxic not only to minorities but just not very nice in general, from regularly belittling my mum and my brother, to women who dare wear leggings—for god's sake. She had married into money and felt that she was a step above most people, but I just found her impossible to tolerate. From then on, it was understood that I would no longer be spending anytime around her.

When my grandma (my dad's mum) died, he called me at work and said he wanted me home to spend the day with him and of course within 10 minutes I was on my way. But when I arrived and his girlfriend tried to join us in the pub, which was a standard Huddersfield way to support the grieving, she tried to join. My dad to my surprise shocked me by saying, "I want to spend time with my daughter which means you are not welcome." It was the first time I had seen him be assertive with her, he actually looked like he was relieved to be able to say something and stand up for me. I was so impressed with him and weirdly we had a great afternoon, considering!

There were times where what he thought (I'm sure) were simple throwaway comments, which haunted me. There was the time when I returned from Australia when I was 18 from a 2 month trip and he said, "Oh bloody hell you're back, I thought you'd love it so much, suit you more that you would find a way to stay."

"Ok so you were quite happy with that...?" No response.

I moved to London and was visited twice in 10 years, both in the latter 5 years when my children were born.

In the first few years of my time in London, I worked lots, travelled lots, partied lots and studied lots. After regularly doing part-time courses at the local college, I fell in love with psychology and made the decision to finally do a university degree. I absolutely loved it but the cognitive psychology elements and residential requirements were quite taxing on my capacity to work full time and support myself. So I called my dad and asked for him to commit to £50 a month support for 1 year so I could ditch a shift to make the time to do better on my coursework. I went in low because it was a token effort of support I was after. London is bloody expensive but anything was better than nothing.

What I got was a tirade of excuses about it not being affordable. He was by no means on the breadline and could easily afford a bottle of whiskey a day, hours in the pub and top of the range refurbishments of his home. What I did get was a goodwill one-off gesture of £25 with a brief note. So I responded with a letter too, which resulted in very little contact for many years.

I basically told him to fuck off. I listed all my accomplishments, from buying a house at 18, to travelling the world, trying to support myself in London while doing a degree, a degree that would have been way more expensive if I had gone for it straight after college. How I asked for very little from him ever and when I had, the refusal was quite hurtful especially when it wasn't for much at all.

I was even in a car accident which apparently he knew about and at no point tried to check in on me. It was just casually brought up about 6 months later during a random and unexpected phone conversation.

I resented not being 'worthy', a recurrent underlying theme throughout my childhood where my mum seemingly had to fight for even the bare minimum child support, whereas his partner lavished more than enough on her children/grandchildren. In retrospect and most definitely am I not giving him credit for this, but as a result my brother and I worked from a young age and became self-sufficient unbelievably early. My dad's partner's own children having numerous financial issues well into their 40s-50s!

He couldn't 'be bothered' travelling to Barbados for my wedding, even when financial assistance was offered. But it was out of term time and not too expensive in reality. Instead I was sent a £500 cheque to put towards it. In true Hazel fashion, I blew it all in one meal at one of the best restaurants in Barbados that originally my then husband and I couldn't justify affording. It all went.

But that doesn't negate the fact that I was embarrassed he didn't come to give me away. His 'father of the bride' speeches are pretty bloody hilarious. I ended up asking a friend to give me away – 'Oh Hazel never does anything normally'. Like it was my choice!

*

What a surprise then that I messed up grieving for my dad too. I positively attributed the hell out of it to rationalise it, justifying my loss and yet again scrape trying to keep my shit together. Due to the rather strained relationship we did have, in the year or so leading up to his death we had reconnected speaking almost daily about my divorce, my kids, his recovery from his recent illness that had hospitalised him. Life in general. I was quite a routine that we would chat on my daily walk home from the gym at lunch that happened quite organically.

Surprisingly for me and yet hugely bloody needed was that he was very concerned for me during my divorce and wanted/needed regular updates on the proceedings and how me and the children were coping. He became quite a regular sounding board. Whether it was a distraction from his pretty distressing 'recovery' or a last ditch attempt to be there for me after coming very close to dying – I don't know. Maybe I was just less combative and clearly needed him which made it easier for him to be there for me.

One day in February, I had quite an important day in court where the proceedings had concluded with what we needed to hear in that my soon to be ex-husband had been told in no uncertain terms that if he didn't stop playing games and agree to my very reasonable offer, the judge would take full control of the divorce outcome which would most definitely be even less so in his favour. This meant that there was very little left to do and the 'fight' was more or less over. I imparted this information to my dad almost immediately after leaving the court and I could sense the relief he felt that I was going to be ok and less 'harangued'.

That evening I went out to dinner to celebrate the worst supposedly being over with. By the time I returned home, my dad had died. I felt completely blind-sided.

However, in the weeks that followed I somehow managed to find coping strategies along the lines of how lucky I was to reconnect before this happened. So much so that it became a mantra for any thoughts in my head or anyone that cared/dared to ask how I was. The more I stated it, the more it worked.

However, I knew from my counselling sessions from the second she mentioned my dad and it was like a sledgehammer to my gut that I may have some unresolved feelings. I'm clever like that! We had to leave it and revisit how this was a prevalent factor in the current state of my mental well-being. Counsellors like to take about our youth and our parents as a starting point in uncovering our issues, it was at least week 6 before I could even vaguely tackle this subject.

It is all linked. And indeed so was how the death occurred, linked to developing my PTSD. Fear of relaxing, getting close to anyone and letting them in at a time in my life where I neither had the capacity nor the willingness to deal with anything other than protecting my children and raising them in the least exposed way to what was happening.

*

When reading Lianna Champ's 'How To Grieve Like A Champ', how she described the grieving process and what is required to process our feelings properly struck such a chord that it shook my whole understanding, yet again, of how naïve my coping mechanisms were/are. I appreciate what was my requirement at the time and retrospect is bollocks. But I recognised what she had to say about delaying or ignoring grief doesn't help it pass. It just buries itself deeper and manifests as depression and unresolved feelings, affecting our capacity to live.

I'm sure that you appreciate that when you bury something deep down, it has to come out at some point. Daring to relax and then being hit with more 'stress' all takes its toll on your psyche.

Chapter Seven
Week 7 – Being an Empath

I'm an empath and it has wreaked havoc with how I have behaved, the situations I have found myself in, what I have tolerated and allowed. It's not an excuse, it's an explanation.

There is quite the difference between having empathy and being an empath. A great article I came across, succinctly describes the issues empath's will often face; 'Common Empath Problems'.

1. Others' emotions can flip yours like a switch.
2. You're constantly battling emotional fatigue.
3. Compassion can feel like a burden.
4. You're torn between going out and staying in.
5. Alone time is necessary – and not everyone understands that.
6. You need time to process transitions.
7. You struggle with anxiety or depression.
8. You know someone is feeling 'off' when no one else notices.
9. People take advantage of your compassion.
10. "Small" things can deeply upset you.

11. Sometimes you forget to leave emotional space for yourself
12. <u>Saying no</u> is really hard.
13. Violence and horror deeply upset you.
14. You don't always know which emotions are yours.

https://highlysensitiverefuge.com/14-problems-only-empaths-will-understand/

We explored why I did this and its repercussions. Why history kept on repeating itself. A lot about counselling and therapy is recognising what we do and why as knowledge is power.

I have been accused of letting people walk all over me on numerous occasions. Firstly, yes I do. Secondly, it's because I've always looked 'outside the box' for why people behave a certain way and therefore not reacted based on my feelings but theirs. So to an outsider, someone's behaviour may have been deemed questionable to say the least and yet I have not been in a position to explain why they may behave a certain way it as that would break a confidence or sound dubious as to why I did understand said actions.

I'm that person who regularly gets chatting to strangers in public, especially those who looks like they are not totally comfortable with the situation they are in (potential dodgy first date) and have found themselves in a compromising position.. Out comes the fake and random long lost friend! Many times I have found myself trapped in dodgy situations where I have struggled to get away and needed a good 'out' myself! I have been known to go above and beyond to help those in similar situations, to help ascertain what is truly going on. Much to the disgust and vitriol of the other person involved!

I end up being confided to about the craziest and shocking of secrets that I then feel duty bound to keep. One actually being the wife (who I barely knew) of a good friend who told me about a 6 years affair she was currently in with another married man. I do have many random numbers in my phone because of this!

Isolated, these can all be ok and quite normal, what is relevant is the frequency and how emotionally invested you get. It's when it affects who you are and how you function that is a problem as it can really take its toll on you mentally, taking on other people's problems and stresses. Regardless of whether they ask you to.

*

I have a strong 'need' to protect people, fix people or fight for the underdog as I know that is what I'd always wanted someone to do for me. To be looked after and made everything ok for, without having to fight. Yet when my 'job is done' that's it, what is left? – And that is completely on me. I get bored or feel no longer required in a relationship that was based on me 'helping' or offering support. When that is no longer a requirement, the relationship often becomes redundant. This does then inevitably leave me with the feeling of being ignored or maybe more accurately, under-appreciated.

But this has ultimately lead me to, whether consciously or not, gravitate towards those that may (in my misguided opinion) need me. Where do I even start with this? Do we fall in love with an emotion rather than a person? Which makes that loves seem less or non-existent once your emotional role in the relationship changes. Very similar to that of 'rebound relationships'.

It is a hugely unhealthy basis for an equal relationship. However, people that recognise this in you will, unfortunately, be able to manipulate you quite easily. Making empath's quite a target for abusive relationships. But we teach people how to treat us.

> *"If you always do what you've always done, you'll always get what you've always got."*
> **– Henry Ford**

I put myself in situations (or definitely used to) where I'm putting myself second at the very best. It's not healthy to constantly treat yourself and your needs as irrelevant or an afterthought. This is my issue, my fault.

I won't stand up for myself enough when I'm berated for something when my retort involves pointing out the truth that would hurt the other person. Or be honest about how I'm feeling if that will cause upset. This has regularly stitched me up. It's very wearing feeling like an emotional punch bag and never standing up for yourself. Eventually you will react and it will be a shock, "Jeez where did that come from!" It will very likely seem disproportionate. Sound familiar?

To understand our needs and what makes us tick is invaluable in terms of being able to make better, more informed decisions. To recognise parts of ourselves that need working on or which are responsible for undesired patterns in our lives.

Although if you do have such a compelling desire to help others, maybe look into doing it as a job. Get paid for what you love to do and be able to set clear boundaries! When your job is done, you are expected to walk away and the 'relationship' is made more equal in terms of what is expected from each other. But a cautionary note must be made in terms of any agenda or motivations in regards to the 'help' and 'advice' you try to offer or indeed in relation to what is received.

On another level, don't automatically discount the option of help from another person because you think they don't understand what you are going through. Those wanting to help may have more insight and a deep rooted and genuine well intentioned reason to reach out.

Chapter Eight
Week 8 – My Childhood

There is so much of my childhood that I find questionable. What I got away with, what I wasn't stopped doing. I was very strong-willed and even from a very young age I was resourceful. I worked from the age of 12 and not just a paper round providing me with an extra tenner a week. It was pub work too and I was averaging £50–80 a week, which I saved a lot of 'for a rainy day'. Which in my world meant, if someone tells me I can't do something, there's very little they can do if I can pay for it myself.

This goes a long way in explaining why I ended up renting my own flat before I'd even reached 17. When you have to ask for money to gain independence, it's a lot harder! My mum was not impressed at all and no doubt looking back, quite embarrassed that I'd chosen to do it.

I recall one evening when I was 16, I'd stayed out all night after working late at my Pizza Hut job in town. This was great fun, hanging out with people a bit older than me. I was in heaven. It also suited me better as I didn't really seem to always get on as easily with people my own age at this time in my life. Hanging out with students in the years above me at school, using fake ID to actually get a job running the bar at a nightclub in town (which ironically ran events in the day too which worked well when not having to explain why I was getting home from working at Pizza Hut so late) which meant these were my peers. Not to forget how fucking hilarious it was when I was serving people who knew I was 2 years below them at school.

I digress, I had started a relationship with one of the Pizza Hut managers, my first real love and it was brilliant! At this point I hadn't yet moved out and my mum (understandably) lost it when I didn't come home one night knowing that I was seeing someone older. He was 25 which seemed thoroughly acceptable and cool. He lived above a greasy spoon I a stumbling distance from the town centre. I felt like such a grown up. I swear to god, I'm so glad I have boys. However, she rocked up at the greasy spoon, barged her way past the counter and waltzed upstairs demanding I came home and 'showed some respect'. Ironically, I claimed her storming into another man's home quite disrespectful. Well, that went down like a cup of cold sick. "While you're living under my roof…"

A week later I chose to live under my own roof with my own rules. Bond, bills, new TV and video player (yes really) purchased all in cash, up front from my savings.

I have operated very similarly throughout my life.

While my friends were 'out out' and getting their hair done, I was in B&Q and Ikea doing up my first home that I owned from the age of 18, then similarly at the age of 23 with the ex-hubs. I isolated myself in doing so, I didn't realise this at the time. Setting myself in good stead would only later lead to jealousy, missing out on 'young stuff' and derision.

Morecambe

Back when I was 12/13 and at high school, quite a few of us went away on an adventure week away staying at an old army base arranged by the school in the glamorous northern town of Morecambe. The plan was to abseil, climb, shoot rifles, archery – you name it. We all stayed in 2 man (women) chalets all lined up, interspersed with various teachers and trainee teachers who were chaperoning.

There was a lot of talk about getting up to no good, sneaking in fags, a dash of booze and who would be 'hanging out' with whom after curfew. Rules are there to be broken, right? My friend and I who were sharing a room had decided this was an excellent idea.

Ever the resourceful one, I did manage to procure the above, as did others, but probably not as successfully as me. A good friend of mine who was quite minted and not coming with us had decanted a whopping amount of Whiskey from her dad's special 20ltr 'on show' and yet already started bottle into a squash bottle for me. I still to this day have no idea if they ever realised that it had been pilfered or not. The toilet roll up the top sealed the deal with my rather extravagant purchase of a 20 pack of Regal Blue from the local petrol station.

I was set, I would be cool. As it turned out, I was even cooler as I had managed to get more than the others. Let's hang out with Hazel and [her room-mate] the awkward gangly girls, they might have been hiding just how insouciantly cool they are all this time. And oh my goodness how addictive that feeling is. We were gobby, flirty, funny and brimming with confidence due to our new found popularity. My confidence boost as well as my slight intoxication helped me thrive at all the activities and garner quite a relationship with the army guys. I was smashing it. Yay me.

Until one night, the others were getting less discreet/over confident with our new found freedom and the teachers and TAs started to suspect something was afoot. We were uncovered as the smoking booze hounds that we were and when push came to shove as to who the ones were leading this debauchery – the fingers were pointed at my chalet. Which consisted of just myself and my best friend (at the time).

What ensued was a good old telling off, naturally. Followed by an additional telling off from a few of the TAs who were understandably very annoyed that their first experience of extra-curricular activities in a high school had resulted in such an occurrence that may reflect badly on their supposed skills as caregivers and authoritarians. Which left us both well and truly in no doubt as to how much trouble we were in. As they left, the panic started to set in. Oh crap we really were in trouble.

As the evening soberly went on (literally), my roomie got more and more anxious about what was going to happen and how her parents would respond. I was not particularly enamoured at the prospect of my first foray in to getting into trouble, that was my brother's speciality but with my roomie there seem to be a panic regarding her parent's response that was more than just a telling off and embarrassment. The tears started and before we knew it, we had hatched a plan that would solve everything. Ahem.

We were going to run away and either hide out in my Grandma's caravan that was nearby or make our own way back to Huddersfield, by which time there would have been enough panic regarding our disappearance that nobody could possibly be upset with us. Such a great plan. Frikkin genius.

What then happened was we set our alarm to wake us at 2am and before it got dark and we had gone to bed, had a look around the fenced off perimeter as to where would be the best way to 'get out', this was an ex-army barracks after all. I found a damaged piece of fence that I was sure we could slip through and made a mental note of where it was, pointers to find it in the dark. And that is what we did. We woke up on time, we left without a sound, and we got through the fence and set off on the 7 mile journey to the seaside town of Morecambe Bay. The journey was 4–5 hours of 2 girls chatting non-stop about life, occasionally stopping to either jump in a bush as a car was coming past or to stop on a random concrete mound in a school playground to have a quick look up at the stars and take in what we had just embarked on. Once we did arrive at our destination the decision was made as the fear set in that as soon as it hit 9am we should phone our parents so that they immediately knew we had not come to any harm and not to worry we would be home soon(ish). How responsible were we? I swear to goodness, kids eh!

But until then there was time to waste, we would pop into 'Bubbles' the swimming place to use the facilities as soon as it opened. We walked up the promenade, checked the opening times of the shops and chatted about our best route home. 9am arrived and our calls to our respective parents were met with a tad more emotion and questions than we had anticipated. Holy crap what had we done. By the time the calls were done, we popped into 'Our Price' music shop as we saw a policeman further down the street and wanted to remain out of sight. Within minutes, we were well and truly surrounded, within an hour we had been returned to the teachers/TAs on our trip and back on the coach in time for the return.

We were both separated and sat next to a teacher each and advised to stay quiet. This would be dealt with at school once there had been appropriate discussions as to how it would be handled.

As you can imagine, we were in a lot of trouble and suitably punished. The teachers involved in the trip from what I gather did not do too well either due to everyone's involvement in getting up to no good and how it was handled. We were despised by the faculty and after numerous comments from the teachers I asked my mum if I could leave. It was not uncommon for me to be bullied at the school anyway and the teachers (so it felt) were now on-board too. There had been interest in an excellent more drama focused school in a different area due to my passion for theatrical extra-curricular activities and as soon as they accepted me, I left. I didn't even tell my friends as they were seemingly enjoying jumping on the bandwagon too. Another barrier, another learned behaviour.

Now don't get me wrong, what we did was stupid, scary and incredibly lucky that we came to no harm in many ways. Another example of me doing the wrong thing for the wrong reasons but with misplaced good intentions at heart. When we are lost, we flail around trying to find a way to be accepted. I had incredibly low self-esteem and the effects of such distort how we behave and see the world. What you do to make yourself seem more appealing as you don't have the faith that you as you is enough. I was pushing boundaries to be noticed. Seemingly protecting my friend. A regular theme I'm sure you will recognise.

I've always been apparently yearning for something more, even as an 8 year old praying for a super win on a packet of Walker crisps to escape to a drama school, a better high school, to excel and explore. The key being to 'Escape'. I've always been painfully shy and always appeared a bit weird – I most definitely did not fit into the mould of what was expected within my family/social circle. I think I kind of wanted a 'do over'! I felt trapped and this would also explain my need to earn from a young age to give me the options I needed, not being limited by funds.

In Will Smith's book 'Will' released in November 2021, there was a line about money and fame solving our problems but how it just serves to further alienates us. This is what I wholeheartedly assimilate with.

*

I was never really comfortable with being hugged as a child even more so by certain people. I was just as stiff as a board, went bright red or made a quick exit. I'm still a bit like this now, although a lot less so from my 30s. I just never really felt comfortable in my own skin. I only really had any form of confidence or less awkwardness when I drank. So when I got to an age where that was possible, I really embraced it!

I've realistically been avoiding the reality of my mental state since I was 13. Being prescribed Prozac at 16, which stayed in my knicker drawer for over 15 years never taken (admittedly said knicker drawer was moved numerous times in regards to the various places I lived). I just struggled with being me and what that entailed.

Being socially awkward can put you in situations that you are not comfortable with and lacking the confidence to say so. Especially if you're in a potential people pleasing situation. The repercussions of going against pack mentality can be very daunting and has caused many an unwanted situation. Some of these sexual and it's easy to learn how popular you can become when you comply.

I have over the years learnt to over compensate with false confidence. The amount of times I have heard that I am so strong and appear to not need anyone really does knock me sideways, even now.

*

I remember once being dumped by pager and taking it like a champ, god forbid I would make a scene and then immediately after experiencing my first ever panic attack. It was politely explained to me once I had called him back as per his pager request in details that I was great, but not as great as the new woman he had met. Rejection was already an issue, but when through thoughtlessness, it really sparked something in me that was hard to control.

This was the $1^{st}/2^{nd}/3^{rd}$ barrier up. This contributed to a mind-set of working on the worst case scenario to prepare myself and not have any surprises my psyche couldn't cope with.

Inevitably when faced with issues of being uncomfortable with who you are and feeling like you are not in control of how people treat you. You search for something you can control. For me, this was my weight. I told myself that maybe I would be more appealing and confident if I was thin and looked good. This is what society tells us, right? Or maybe unconsciously I was just trying to get attention, give people the chance to show that they were worried and cared. I possibly wasn't that 'good' at it, but at least I thought I was and that was what mattered at the time, I guess.

Until one day I was out with my work lot in a pub dancing the night away, I was 17 and as had become my Modus Operandi, they were predominantly at least 10 years older than me, I think I found it less threatening. One of the women took me to one side and asked me when the last time I had a period was. I knew she was going through quite a hard time with fertility issues and she pointed out that her current issues were down to how dangerous her eating disorder had got at my age. How she was now paying the price and before it got too late I should really take into consideration the implications of the route I was apparently going down. This hit me like a brick. It struck the right chord with me as I knew children were always going to be on my agenda. But then again, it could have just been that I had succeeded in getting noticed.

That in no way stopped it immediately in its tracks, issues were had for a good 20 years or so at varying times, but it stopped it getting worse and has made me more mindful of what is ultimately important. It may be a 'go-to' but I'm lucky that it does not completely take over to an extent that I make myself ill.

*

Another good example of my failure to comply with social norms is back when I was 18 and my love of travelling on my own. My poor mother! However, on one particular instance my Grandma decided that she fancied coming along for the ride too on a trip I'd arranged to South East Asia. We got on like a house on fire so it was an immediate yes from me, all I did do was change my flights to a slightly less dingy airline to make it more pleasant for her as she was 76, but she was by no means a stranger to travel and adventure.

The family were somewhat against it. Evidently I/we were being irresponsible – especially at her age. Pah, she was more able and adventurous than all her daughters put together when she was 76. I suspect jealousy may have been at play. Even though it wasn't uncommon for my Grandma to jet off to Australia for 2 months incorporating visiting my uncle and his family, (her son) while in Queensland. Even before my Grandad died she would leave him at home so she could truly escape and enjoy herself. She was so ahead of her time!

Within a month or so, we embarked on just short of a month travelling to Kuala Lumpur, through to the Perhentian Islands followed by a road trip through to Surat Thani to veer left towards Phuket stopping at Khao Sok National Park for some serious jungle time. Loving it so much that we didn't actually make it to Phuket before heading back towards Surat Thani to get the boat over to Khoa Tao and Ko Pha Ngan (Half Moon Party!) for a few days in each before we finished up our trip un Bangkok. The first few days of which was on the famous Khao San Road to soak in the crazy atmosphere while finishing off our trip in a nice 'real' hotel before we headed back to reality.

The trip was incredible. My grandma was the epitome of independent. If she fancied joining me on a trip round an island trialling a moped she did, if she fancied reading a book or going for a solo walk, she did. At times, she wanted to immerse in the more in-depth historical elements of the culture while I embraced the massage school's offerings at The Kings Palace. We chatted to so many people along the way and completely immersing ourselves in our adventure. Unique as the pairing appeared to some, for us it worked fantastically. We even had some backpackers that we met on the boat trip from Surat Thani near the Malaysian border who delightedly spotted us in the heart of Bangkok a week later and some 640km away shouting, "Hey it's Hazel and Grandma!" We stayed in huts on the beach, Treehouses on the rocky cliffs of Koh Tao, snorkelled with turtles, ate incredible street food costing pennies and hit Hard Rock café for ridiculously priced wine!

When we begrudgingly went home to grumpy partners and normality, it was noted by some of the family who were originally against our trip away that my Grandma did indeed look very well after the holiday. A compliment, blink and you missed it though.

There is so much that happens in our lives. There are memories that mean something and those that don't. Time passed is often irrelevant. This is one of my favourites.

*

Let's Give A Big Hurrah To All The Strong Women Out There
2 March 2016

What is a strong woman to you? Is it how much they have achieved in work, family, financially, what they have been through and survived or how they tackle every day and/or unpredictable issues that life frequently throws at us? There are so many ways to be strong, this is what it means to me...

Being strong comes in so many forms and is hugely important to me, as I'm sure it is to you too. Who do you admire? I'm lucky in that I'm spoilt for choice, although none of them for the same reason.

There is my grandma, who has lived an incredible life. At the ripe young age of 90, she has rowed for Cambridge, been a magistrate, founded charities for 'Concern for Mental Health', backpacked all over the world (including a 4 week stint around Malaysia and Thailand with me when I was 18), cooks the best Chocolate fudge cake going, oh and did I mention, she also raised 4 children.

Following the death of my Grandad over 9 years ago, whom she tirelessly looked after for 50+ years (in them there days). Slowly, what many people in their later years dread, she developed Alzheimer's and Dementia. Nasty and cruel diseases that often go hand in hand, that can often make an already daunting a lonely time of your life, more so. She knows she has it, she accepts that she rarely knows what she is supposed to be doing, who with and when. She has 20 minute cycles before she is confused and suspects she is making her 'problem' obvious. The more she panics the worse it gets.

She is very bright and knows relatively well how to cover up her mistakes and that her memory from 20 years + is as affected as yours and mine (meaning she can regain clarity by reminiscing on her younger years). On top of this, it upsets her, you can see it in her face, that she doesn't remember my children. But she keeps asking as this is important to her, to know, even if it does mean displaying her weakness.

Completely on a different scale, there are the famous ones; Amy Poehler (absoflippinglutely funny as hell, clever, a mother, hardworking, divorced) Holly Willoughby (gorgeous, funny, successful and yet manages to have seemingly no enemies, how refreshing), Amy Schumer (doesn't give a crap, gets on with it her way and succeeding incredibly), Malala Yousafzai (this is obviously not in order, such courage and conviction)—I could go on for some time. In my opinion, a strong woman to be admired is the woman who strives for independence and/or is independent and yet has the humility to not assume she is infinite. To know we have flaws rather than projecting your issues on to somebody else and yet doesn't give a crap what others think about you. Real strength is in knowing whose opinion matters and knowing how and when to be honest. A cracking sense of humour, to be witty and know how to laugh at yourself.

Every now and again, I think it helps to reflect on what matters to you. To not take people for granted just because you are 'used to' how impressive they are. To acknowledge what makes them great and learn, you don't have to admire people from afar, you can be proud of yourself too.

Chapter Nine
Week 9 – Stalking

'Past relationships and patterns'

So, I've had a few stalkers, some minor and some fucking scary as hell. All of which have contributed to who I am and how I behave, how I have learned to normalise it to not be running scared. Or extra procedures that I put in place to ensure my safety. Some that I'm sure I am even oblivious to or have become second nature. All we experience shape who we are.

There was the one that I went on one date with when I was 15 and he came on way to strong, I felt uncomfortable and not even slightly attracted to him, I made an excuse and left. As I was only 15, I was attending drama lessons every Tuesday evening 5–6pm in a village at the other side of Huddersfield to where I lived called Lindley, I made my own way there after school and often got picked up at the end by my mum. The guy I had a date with found out where I was at this time and one day I came down the steps from the studio to see him waiting for me under the stairs. This shook me up and definitely took me by surprise but I just shouted something clumsily along the lines of 'oh crap, oh no, I'm really busy I have to run – mum's waiting for me'. The next week he was there again but the dad of the kid after me with my drama teacher interrupted and said, "By the way there is a very dodgy looking guy down there hiding under the stairs is he anything to do with you?" I pointed out that he'd been there last week as well. They were a tad surprised that I'd not told anyone. A theme I guess of not appreciating the seriousness. They walked me down to the bus stop and said that from now on its best I got picked up directly from the car park. For a few weeks, both the dad and my tutor made a point of escorting me down after my lesson and eventually he got bored and stopped appearing. Different times eh?

Then there was the one that I met in a bar after work in Leeds, at a popular student bar, a barge called 'The Dry Dock'. Balls out amazing fun, especially if you're 17. Although I didn't attend University in the conventional way, I tried to experience as much as possible and it did help working at Pizza Hut with so many students and those who just love a piss up (me).

I got chatting to a guy who from what I could see was a fun guy, but half way through the evening I'd got bored as he was really clingy so I tried to do a runner. He caught up with me and declared that we were 'Sympatico' or some such nonsense so to get rid of him I gave him my fake phone number.

To be honest I was quite surprised I hadn't given him my real number as I can be a bit 'special' at times, especially after £1 a pint Wednesdays.

The next day at work, a few of them were commenting about the scary guy who kept glaring at me whenever I walked away or spoke to anyone else. I was like, "I thought he was ok, no? I did get a bit bored." He was very pissed evidently when I left and got escorted out of the pub. Well done, Haze, great work! But then a few days later at work I had my boss have a go at me for having people calling me at work. To be fair it wasn't a huge deal, but the boss in question liked being a bit off with any of the younger girls . She said that my dad wanted to know what time I finished so he could pick me up, she had told him and told me that in future make sure I get my going home arrangements sorted out of work hours. I pointed out to my friends on shift that there is not a chance in hell that my dad called and certainly wouldn't be picking me up. That she was either making it up or I should be a bit worried. Sure as hell, the guy from the Dry Dock was waiting for me after work on the bench at my finish time. Quite convinced I would be ok with the arrangements by the looks of it, lucky my two Adams were there 6 foot (at least) a piece and frog marched me to the pub. It was a joke that I had to pee as quickly as them or they were coming in to get me in case 'crazy eyes' had come back to get me. I learnt to pee quickly and so was born the routine of regularly drinking with them after work, y'know for safety reasons. I ended up buying my first house with one of them.

Next up, there was the time in New York and was approached by a guy who saw me looking at a tourist map (I can't stress how much this is a bad idea, I try my best to never look lost or too much like a tourist ever since. Stubbornly so!) He asked if I needed help and struck up a conversation where I got myself into a situation where I didn't want to be rude or for the 6ft 6 Haitian guy to take offence to my abruptness. So I just said, "Listen I'm tired, thank you for your help I'm just going to chill and get a drink and plan my day." This way I would be in a bar and be 'safer'. "Sounds great, I'll join you."

Oh fuck. "Oh ok." Double fuck. I'd just duck out when he went to the toilet or something. I managed to spout some bullshit that enabled me to exit without being rude, why the hell I was so bothered was bonkers, but I've always felt safer feeling I was placating people.

Now New York is a pretty big place with a shit load of people so that should have been the end of it. Weirdly not. I kept thinking I'd seen him and I did spot him in the Time Square Starbucks at one point and did a runner. So I decided to spend the day in a completely different part of Manhattan. While getting of the Staten Island ferry, I got a call from a good friend back home saying that his brother was in town and did I fancy catching up and keeping him company? Sounds like a good plan considering I thought I might have got myself some unwanted attention. So we went out and got smashed. Obviously.

Turns out he was a lawyer for Barclays brokering a deal for some aviation thing and his expenses were great fun to play with. We ended up back at his hotel, The Waldorf Astoria which is a step up from sharing a room with 12 other people at Columbia University's hostel digs. We ordered more beer and Pizza, passing out god knows when. When I woke up, he left the address of his offices just a couple of blocks away with a note to say pop in and say hi when I get up. I did, but it didn't last long as I was there about 5 minutes before I felt the fear sink in of how crap I felt and I needed to get out before I embarrassed myself. So I left a nicely air conditioned building for NYC in the summer heat. Which works wonderfully with a hangover. I panicked and headed straight for the huge Easynet (Internet café by the EasyJet people, back when we didn't get the net on our phones!), just on Times Square in search of the cold. I got in and felt a wave of relief immediately, and almost immediately after I felt sick got up to try and find somewhere to throw up and bam – I passed out.

By the time I was coming around, people were helping me up and getting me into a cab. As we were driving away, I said to the driver, "Oh crap you need to know where you're going."

"No, the guy who put you in told me where to go and paid your fare. Columbia University right?"

Ok. Turns out that was a very tall black man, which was all I got. When I got into the hostel, I asked if I'd had any dodgy visitors or messages and they confirmed that a guy had been trying to get in and get details about me, see when I was back, etc. They said they had strict policies on who could enter if they weren't staying there or giving guest details out (unless they paid the $12 for a bed in a shared room obvs) and to watch myself as it looked dodgy and recommended finding somewhere different that he didn't know about.

I went to Hooters that night with some of the guys from my dorm so I was in a group and obviously to go to Hooters! I left the next morning to stay at a hostel near Madison Square Gardens, 70 blocks away and I was very careful when I left!

Weirdly about 8ish years later I found a random message on my Facebook, in the message section where people you're not connected to can try and speak to you (?) and there he was saying 'hi, remember me?' Holy crap.

*

Then we have the one where he tried to kill me. I moved out of my family home at the ripe old age of 16. There were a mixture of reasons in addition to my stroppiness, but one of them was that I was in the town centre and therefore it was easier to get to college in Leeds and home from working late without taxis, or even later nights waiting around etc. Let's be honest, it wasn't an incredible place or even location, but it was 5 minutes' walk from the train station so it was really handy. There was however a rather secluded (for late at night) bridge that I needed to go under. After a few months, I was starting to feel like I was being followed. Seemingly the same guy picking up on my walk at the corner of The George Hotel next to the train station. My rather blasé response to this was to always call my mum and have her chat to me while I walked back, assuming that me describing who was behind me and having some sort of a witness being sufficient (my poor mother, but I was not to be told!).

Then, when I was actually in my flat which had direct access to the road and my own driveway, on 2 occasions I was trapped in my flat as the lock had been jammed by someone (supposedly) trying to break in. Then finally, one morning my then boyfriend (one of the Adams) who regularly stayed over left at 7am to get to work and 10 minutes after he called me quite shook up saying that he'd had an accident as the brakes on his new car had failed completely. Luckily as it was early and the roads were quiet nobody was hurt, he'd used the curb to buckle his tyres and reduce his speed. Thank god he was driving as I'd only been driving a month or so and would not have had the faintest idea what to do.

When we got the car towed to the Citroen garage, the car still being under warranty, they informed us that the brake cable had been quite obviously cut. They handed it to us, kind of like a souvenir. I honest to god still have it now! The police were called and we explained that it wasn't an isolated incident and what could/would they do? We were told that just around the corner from me was a new site for housing refugees and the area was increasingly less safe (wow) and as I'm young and blonde I may have caught their eye, having a new car was probably not working in my favour either. I shit you not. He, the policeman then proceeded to ask me if I was set on staying living there as it really looked like it wasn't safe for me there anymore. That was that.

'Luckily' I had a 2 month trip to Australia booked setting off very soon after, so we packed up my whole flat within 24 hours and stayed with my mum for the remaining time until I left and gave notice to my landlord.

*

Now, this next one is a pretty messed up and by far my worst. Back in the early 2000s to supplement my various acting and modelling jobs I worked in the local bars and restaurants. Great tips, access to free drinks/food and flexibility with shifts, perfect. One of the bars was in Teddington, a great local where it was frequented by the middle class locals, crew from Teddington Studios and largely manned by those on travelling stop-gaps. It was rare that we went straight home after our shift. Either a lock-in or hitting a club or house party. On one of the lock-ins, a few of the locals joined in, 2 of which were men that always came in to the pub together and funnily enough as men in their mid-40s they liked hanging out with younger people, especially the girls. Shock.

After copious amounts of tequila, one of them was showing me quite a bit of attention. It was funny and intriguing but I wasn't paying too much attention in return. Predominantly because after 6 months of 'barmaid chat' I still didn't know which was which and didn't want them to know, they were good tippers. However, just as the night was coming to an end one of them planted a kiss on me, I declared my taxi had arrived and ducked out. Initially I found it hilarious and quite a fun/shocking story to tell. But then he was still a regular that I would be seeing... And I still didn't know whether he was Mike or Mark.

This made life interesting for a few weeks when he came in. I'm prone to blushing at the best of times and that mixed with my lack of interest and especially if he found out I didn't know who he was, awkward avoidance made me some kind of challenge I guess. This was his Achilles heel.

Slowly but surely his attention, conversation and humour made things a bit less awkward and eventually I agreed to have a proper drink with him sometime. This guy was very bright and so quick witted it was quite a thrill. Everywhere we went was fun and unique, he seem to take my knack of talking to random strangers and notch it up 1000% for himself. He was fearless, well connected, charismatic, oh and rich. You somehow felt more interesting and enigmatic, even funnier in his company. His ability to get people to talk about the most intense and personal parts of their life was fascinating, until it wasn't of course.

Within a few months, to my surprise we were in a relationship and having a blast. Private members clubs/restaurants, the races with his own horse (obvs), weekends abroad, test driving Aston Martin's, the lot. I'd met his son, knew all his work colleagues and staff, his friends and knew quite a bit about his rather dysfunctional upbringing.

But then the warning signs started seeping in. First there was the lady who came in to work and told me that she was sleeping with him too and he'd given her chlamydia so I should get checked out. I found this quite shocking as he was so balls out 'in to me' so I thought it was an ex possibly causing trouble and confronted him about it. To my utter surprise he threw it back at me saying that 'adult' relationships were complicated and there was a bit of an overlap, especially as initially I'd been reluctant to commit properly. My fault. Also, thanks a bunch for quite obviously me being the source of the chlamydia and how embarrassing it was for him. This was my cue to distance myself and get out. We were over and I was ok about it. It was fun while it lasted but the way he threw that back at me made me feel quite gobsmacked and confused.

I ignored various texts and kept as much distance while he was in the bar as possible. He then upped the ante by claiming his son was missing me and have I finished having my childish tantrum yet?

Very 'you're such a silly girl but I still love you, let's at least be friends as we have so much fun'. I can't completely explain it, but he had a great way of making me feel like I was being the unreasonable one. When hanging out as friends ("because that is what grown-ups do c'mon Hazel I thought you were more mature than that"), the charm was turned on, the raucous nights with high-end wine at the chef's table while others commented on our 'hilarious chemistry' slowly morphed back into a relationship that I honestly can't say when it actually happened. It was just assumed, seemingly without my knowledge. He won as many of my friends over with either giving them jobs, free flowing drugs , picking up the bar tab and supposed insightful wit.

However shortly after, anyone not on board with being bought were undermined and ridiculed. "He fancies you, are you going to let him treat me like that? Why does she hate you so much, the way she looks at you haven't you noticed?" Etc. He also tried it on with a few of my friends 'to test their loyalty'.

Then the stalking started. I was getting 40–50 calls a day. The calls would start when I turned my light on in my bedroom, if I finished a shift early at work and to my boyfriend's annoyance when I was spending an evening in with him. This caused many fights; was it a secret boyfriend trying to get in touch with me? Crazy ex's who were not happy I was in a new relationship? Was I giving my number out to random men? The answer to this was him constantly requesting I changed my number to cut old people off. I have had the same number since I was 16.

Further reasons for what was happening, was explained to me that it was due to how I look at men, making them think I was in love with them. Or women for how I made them feel because of how I looked at men. It was regularly pointed out to me when I was 'doing it' so I used to get nervous and try and avert my eyes. As a 22 year old woman who had had a few stalkers already, I wasn't about to be bullied into disconnecting from a phone that all my old friends had as well as old work modelling and acting contacts. I honestly didn't want to miss out on the work. Nor was some creep going to scare me into it. I started to suspect my boyfriend as the calls were definitely worse when I wasn't with him, he was obviously showing worryingly controlling behaviour and this ended coming up in a row which resulted in such a fit of rage that he threw a portable air conditioning unit at me. He stormed out of the house, I gathered my things and left.

Later that evening he 'pocket dialled' me and I could hear him and a friend quite obviously having a party with 2 other women at his apartment. It drove me mental that so soon after our argument he was 'getting it on' and I actually drove to outside his place to prove to myself that it was actually happening. Sure enough, his balcony doors were open and I could hear everything. Again, this was what I needed to confirm that enough was enough.

I have read so many stories similar to this where you can't comprehend how much some mug is putting up with, but honestly, until you are in it, it is hard to explain the thought processes.

Especially when coercive control is involved.

However, it probably isn't a surprise to hear that the pocket dial was not an accident. It was intentional to show me how it feels for him when I'm not with him. Do I understand now and will I stop being so selfish?

What I do need to point out is that when our relationship started, I was living with 4 of my friends, all of which were male. It was great fun and we all worked in the hospitality industry, so late nights and free booze were a regular. This contributed to his jealousy and 'worries'. I did eventually move out and got a 2 bed flat with a friend of mine, the time was right and the hope was that the jealousy and accusations would stop. Ha!

He asked to come over to our flat one night after another argument to drop my things off, I asked for my friend to be there as backup/to ensure I wasn't talked into doing something crazy like admitting it was all my fault and fall at his mercy. He came over as planned, it was frosty and weird and he asked for something of his back. I can honestly not remember what it was but it involved me going to my room. While I was in there, something dismissive was shouted and the door slammed. Immediately my flatmate and I stood there like 'what the actual fuck'. For the next, god knows how long we talked about how mental he was, thank god I'm out of it (again) etc. We had a bit of a giggle at his expense with the odd glib comment of 'well he was good for expensive booze and drugs though right', as you do. We went out and hit the pub.

Then the texts started, relaying our whole conversation of what we'd said after he left, but of course he hadn't. He'd slammed the door and hid in our coat closet by the door and heard everything. Fuck. On so many accounts.

But now he had what he wanted, a guilt stick to beat me with. The tears, threats and shame thrown at me. I really didn't like being on my own with him as he had this bizarre power over me that is hard to explain precisely but he could make me feel heartless and broken if I didn't respond kindly to him. Kindness meant hope and forgiveness.

Months passed of the same tumultuous nonsense that got more unfathomably acceptable. Friends were losing patience with me, so much that I was embarrassed to say when crazy shit happened. The calls continued, still obviously at times of the day as a result of being watched. When I woke up (light on in my room), when I finished work… The police were notified, who recorded it as an issue but could do very little until I was attacked. I know – wtf! The pleas from him to ditch my phone number and move in with him so he can protect me got incessant and accusatory.

Then there was the night that I was sitting on his sofa and the calls started as he was putting his laundry away. But in the reflection from the oven glass door I could see the tell-tale blue screen light shining out from the laundry cupboard as my phone was ringing. It was him all along. I got up so quickly and grabbed the bed sheet to send the phone flying. "Oh my god it was you all along."

"Of course it was you silly girl."

This all seems quite bizarre and obviously wrong. But it is very hard to think as clearly when you are in it. One of the many reasons 'they' get away with it, it the believability factor, being perceived quite differently by other people, already wearing you down. Exhaustion plays a huge role. Not to mention already been isolated from those that were your biggest supporters.

Rather paradoxically, as well as going back to him, repeatedly. I also showed too much fight at times. When he locked me out of his apartment and went away for days without any notice, I couldn't get my things, things I needed. He liked the element of control. However, I borrowed the ladder from the pub next door and simply broke in. I learnt when the vitriolic abuse was hurled to not respond no matter how hurtful what he said was, this way my response could not be thrown back at me as 'irrational'. I feigned subservience when having one of his digs or 'episodes' in precarious situations, such as if I was alone with him abroad, at a dinner with just his friends or when his son was in the next room. My resolve seemed to panic him that he was losing his touch. His constant new tactics were getting crazier and starting to show him losing it.

Then he got very ill while on a weekend away just after the penny finally dropping that I no longer had the energy to care what he said or did to me. He was rushed to hospital and remained there for a week in quite a bad way. It was the most relaxing week ever for me, in part I suspect because I felt numb to his games. I visited sparingly, predominantly to make sure he was there and bloody staying there but also not to be seen to leaving him high and dry in such a bad way. The guilt trip factor. He got as many people such as his ex's to visit when he knew I was due to make me jealous but he could see that it didn't bother me one iota. He could see whatever he used to have over me was broken.

When he was finally discharged, I drove him home and told him that I would be collecting my things for good, but I wished him well. As we entered his home (at this point a new place that he had bought supposedly for us), there must have been a glimmer of hope that seeing just how stunning it was would pull on my heartstrings or my love of swanky stuff . It did not. I went to the bedroom to grab my final bits and as I was emptying the bedside table he flew at me. It all happened so quickly but before I knew it, his pillow was over my head and he was just pushing. I scrabbled for anything, luckily I clasped onto the bedside lamp and swung it at him. I got just enough of time to grab my phone and run to the bathroom, lock it and phone the police.

It felt like within seconds they were121on speakerphone and negotiating with him, calming him, telling him that they were minutes away. I was so high on adrenaline I was begging them to help me leave and be able to get out now. They explained that all that was happening was being recorded and would he let me leave? His reputation was everything to him and this appealed to something else in him. He assured them that he was away from the door and I ran like the clappers. He obviously refused to open the electric gate, but quite frankly I climbed it like Spider-Man and was over in no time. The police pulled over and rescued me as I was running down the road asking a complete stranger to help me.

There are a lot of situations throughout this relationship that I could tell you about, but these are just a few to give you a picture of what goes on in such situations.

So yes, that was probably my worst one.

*

A note on coercive control

Those at the hand of Coercive Control may notice that what they experience is so far-fetched or situations/experiences have so isolated you that there was no way or anyone who you could explain to what you are going through.

There is so much more knowledge, understanding and realisation of the varying forms of abuse that we may have endured and yet at the time, due to lack of understanding, it just caused confusion, fear and anything and everything – you name it. The increased knowledge can help us to come to terms with what has happened in the past or may even still be enduring. It does offer the possibility to form paths to recovery instead of thinking that you were to blame or are somebody you are not. Somebody you were incessantly told you were to bring you down or attribute blame.

For more details, please get professional help and advice. https://www.womensaid.org.uk/information-support/what-is-domestic-abuse/coercive-control/

I know I want to find someone who doesn't want to put me through the ringer to prove how much control they have. To just be. To be loved unconditionally. Not to see me as a challenge, someone to tame or mould into what they think I should be.

*

Now this next incident I can honestly say I have no proof whatsoever as to who the guy potentially was. All I can state is the striking resemblance and coincidence, which honestly only dawned on me years later.

Back when I was 21, I had a rather hilarious night out with my work buddies that resulted in a fractured foot in numerous places as a result of some 'interesting' dancing. I'm so clever. This made working in the restaurant industry and catwalk work pretty hard and I had to get creative. My solution was to become a Tequila Girl. Obviously. You can make a lot of money in one night and therefore maximise your earning potential in the least time possible on your feet.

I would generally work one weekend night and bring home a few hundred quid, resting my foot as much as possible the rest of the time. I would use my crutches to get to the assigned venue, then hide them while I was on shift. Willingly taking the offer of letting a guy buy me one of my own shots, a win-win. More profits and pain relief. Us women and multitasking eh?

This did mean that I was often on the N22 night bus getting off at the same stop at the same ungodly hour, trundling along on crutches. I then lived in Twickenham and my stop was on the Green with a 5 minute hobble home.

One evening as I got off the bus, I immediately sensed a car start up that was just for some reason on my radar so I slowed down to give him (I'd assumed) the chance to go past, but he did not. What he did do was slow down, wind the window down and ask about my leg and how I'd hurt it. I tried to just get on with my walk home without being rude or dismissive (reader, women do this way too much).

"Oh this, it's nothing, I have a crutch in case I need it but it's almost healed, thank you."

"Let me give you a lift." As he is crawling alongside me in his silver people carrier.

"No thank you."

"Don't be silly, I'm a cabby. I'd just prefer to see you home."

"I really am good; I just live here." (Pointing to a near, on street, well-lit house)

"Jeez, you women won't accept help will you?"

"We don't always need it."

What I then heard (or not) was a disgruntled retort, window shot up and he sped off.

I always remembered that night as it just felt off. How I was cautious of not aggravating him and at the same time assessing my surroundings in case he got out of his car, as he was not a small bloke. The way his demeanour changed when he knew he wasn't getting his way. How I was walking in case

I needed to get a sturdy stance to use my crutch if needed. How much my foot hurt and how helpful a lift would have been...

These incidents are not that uncommon to some people I'm sure and I also think there are men out there that would genuinely stop to try and offer 'assistance' not quite appreciating the precariousness of the time and location. I'm not a stranger to certain situations as we have read above, all of which made me a tad blasé to 'things that happen'. It was not until years later that a documentary came out about the murder of Milly Dowler. Marsha McDonnell and Amelie Delegrange, how Levi's Bellfield tried to ingratiate himself, especially in regards to Milly from what we know. How he looked. The car he reportedly drove and most importantly how his victims looked.

For those that aren't aware, Bellfield's 3rd victim, Amelie Delegrange was killed within months of the incident above on her way home from a night out, on Twickenham Green.

Chapter Ten
Week 10 –My Dodgy 'Humour'

Oh the laughs we had.

This was discussed at length. It feels like it should be irrelevant but it isn't. I have used it as a defence mechanism for as long as I can remember. To bat away attempts at mocking me or taking me for granted. Or when I haven't understood a situation properly and didn't want to look dumb. To stave off the potential let down – god forbid I will admit I have been hurt or humiliated. It's not all to save face, sometimes I need it for myself. Managing my own expectations as when I break or feel sad, I scare myself.

This does quite often involve 'inappropriate' humour. When asked whether I'm scared about getting married quite young to a particular kind of person, "I'm doing it for the gym membership and PMI, my work benefits are shite" most definitely wasn't the most honest of responses. But when the inevitable humiliation came, surely that lessened how much of a mug I looked?

I've used my 'humour' to shock people, to put them on the back foot when they've hurt me. Textbook passive aggressive but with an added layer of 'does she mean it or did she actually say that?' Testing the boundaries, which is ironic as it normally happens when boundaries have been tested. I've heard regularly that people have said, 'ah yes it's just Hazel, she's fucking with you'. Ironically in my mind I was creating a situation where my flippancy was used to not cause a ruckus, to not show I'm hurt but also not to add to 'other people's issues'. Don't worry about me, I've got thick skin.

Sometimes it's done just to see if they're my kind of people. But we are aware of only 5% of our actions and 95% is completely left to the therapists to decipher. Why do we do what we do? Should we be to blame for the 95%? Not exactly, but we do have a responsibility to understand what we are putting out there. The Americans and their way of using a therapist like we do a toothbrush might be on to something.

I do and have always had problems with letting people in. I know that in the past my lack of assertiveness has created precarious situation for me. If you don't let them in, you don't need to assert yourself when you are upset as it matters less.

Yet then again, with a sarcastic sense of humour (a northern sense of humour no less) how are they to know when something matters? Arguably you could say that those close to you should know, but humans are inherently lazy with their emotions, especially the British!

What is hard is recognising the areas you need to improve for your sanity and work on having more honest relationships with those that knew you before you recognised you needed to change and maybe even kind of liked it! We don't always need to change, maybe we need to fine tune or accept who it is we are trying to please.

But ultimately this was something I was letting people use as a reason to disregard me. However, if we don't put our needs first and respect ourselves, how can we expect others to?

I've spent a lot of my time wondering what I did to make people think I deserved a lot of things in my life. Why they cared so little. Is my honesty too real – is it real? Am I too obnoxious and standoffish (trying to push them away before they choose to)? Why do I let people take advantage and use me? Is it because I make it easy for them?

I think I behave a certain way to keep people at arm's length, so they can't hurt me. How uncomfortable it is or can be for people to be nice and supportive. I guess that depends on the person, their background, own issues and beliefs. Life is rarely simple. Low self-esteem can also make us paranoid.

*

Defence systems – I was so defensive about letting the 'black dog' in, like I was teetering on the edge since my first real dalliance with anxiety and depression when I was 16. Dodging it in any way possible. I somehow knew once it was unleashed, it would be torrential. I remember watching a TV programme once where it showed the decline of someone's mental health as a result or how events played out and how we're all possibly a few mistakes, accidents or situations away from 'losing it'. It rung so true and I'll never forget that moment that made me realise how close I could be. It scared me as I knew (or thought) people only like me when I'm strong. Resilience is key, right?

I do have a thing about positive attribution. My need to find reasons to make all outcomes workable. Constantly looking for negativity, ironically, in a good situation in case it fails so that the drop is less severe.

"If he cheats, it's better than him just not loving you anymore and you'll have more time to learn Japanese and travel"

"If you get that dream job, you won't have the time to see 'x, y and/or z' through"

"If your friend ditches you, do you remember that time they really let you down? See, it's a good thing."

If you're laughing, you're not sad, right? If you're making fun of yourself, it's less fun for others to do it, right? If I can take the piss out of a dodgy situation more than anyone else, surely that renders their attempt a bit dull…

Ultimately, this is a cop out and very damaging. Once we broke down why I was really behaving like this it helped me to appreciate how it was contributing to how people treated me. If you make out that your feelings are a joke, if you belittle your own experience of what has happened to you or what you are going through – you teach people how to treat you. You make it harder for people to understand how to approach you and understand you. Or make it easier for those who can't be arsed, to disregard you.

Slowly over the course of the last few years I have been working on being more honest with myself and those that mattered. To show vulnerability when you are genuinely upset or not coping. Yes I still make jokes, especially inappropriate ones but I'm more cautious as to who they are aimed at, why and how they may make me look.

An inability to show vulnerability isn't necessarily regarded as strength, it just makes you unapproachable or hard to identify with, alienating ourselves further.

Chapter Eleven
Week 11 – Bullying

There is so much in regards to what I have already told you about that contributes to explaining why I ended up on the end of unwanted behaviour towards me. I make it too easy.

Writing this book was also about me focusing and using my experiences to shine a light on why certain people are targeted, further become easier targets and how to find peace or excel rather that constantly deal with the repercussions. I find, unfortunately, that when you are used to being bullied you tend to be nice to people who don't deserve it to hopefully stop anymore, which can be perceived as weak or a walkover.

Being an empath means I stand up for the underdog, but I don't want to stand up for myself when mistreated. That would often involve throwing somebody else under the bus and I don't 'play the game'. The secrets I've kept to protect others and because it didn't sit well with me breaking a confidence are ridiculous.

It's common knowledge among those that know me that I am regularly bullied or targeted for abuse and vitriol. When I have asked them to be honest as to why and whether they think it's ok, I've had responses such as:

"But look at you, you're every woman's nightmare, you can't blame her." That will be my fake confidence then.

"I don't think people understand you and are threatened by you, when they get to know you they'll back off." My dodgy humour. My oblivion to how much of a feminist I was.

"You do put yourself is dubious situations..." Being an empath. Horrific dating decisions.

People who are intimidated by you talk bad about you in the hope that others won't find you so appealing.

I have always worked hard to form my path in life, nothing was ever handed to me. My parents weren't rich. Both my brother and I knew that if we wanted anything, we needed to work for it. However, the very sad fact of our society is that when a man owns a home from a young age and has an element of financial independence, they are hard-working. When it comes to women, the immediate assumption is a sugar daddy or screwing someone over in a divorce. A stance from both men and women.

There are different expectations of women, those daring to even slightly stray from the norms are trouble makers. Or they highlight what is possible and that scares people. The more acceptable it comes for women to be less tolerant of the boxes they are put in the more people have to address their own shortcomings and excuses for maintaining status quo for the sheer ease of it. "These women are chaotic. We must vilify them and halt this."

*

I was raised by a single mum who just got on with things and my father was relied on for very little. If my mum wanted to make her house look like how they did in all the magazines, she learnt how to sow using off cuts from Skopos (even the name brings back memories of trawling through remnant cloths and dodgy seconds). It was rare that she had just one job and she was very resourceful. We got to regularly go on holiday by mum's keen skills to find a stupidly cheap holiday on teletext, so long as we were ready to go with an hour's notice. On a few occasions, she came and collected my brother and me early from school, interrupting our current class to take us out after quickly running it by the teachers. Off to Benidorm we would go – £200 all in with a half-board slightly dodgy hotel. The good old days eh!

She got her degree once we were old enough to give her more free time to do so and formed quite a career in Early Years education, her skills hugely sought after that even saw her being invited to No. 10.

My Grandma as previously mentioned was quite an influence in my life and her attitude was one that I just grew up with and was normal to me. A mother of 4 children, born in the 1920s, with a grumpy, less than approachable husband (putting it mildly/delicately) resulting in separate rooms from before I can ever remember. She developed an independent life, one that fulfilled her regardless.

She was a rower in the Oxford-Cambridge University Boat Race. A magistrate. A mental health worker at the local hospice. On the board at the local hospice. A Director and key worker for the charity 'Concern for Mental Health' in Huddersfield back in the 80s for many years. Traipsing around Huddersfield every Thursday making sure that anyone who they were helping who needed it, got a lift to a weekly meeting in a church in Slaithwaite where they were fed a hearty home cooked meal and entertained.

She still worked a full shift at my Aunt's café every Wednesday to ensure she got a day off. Travelled extensively. Was ridiculously fit well into her 70s and quite weirdly still had time to make copious amounts of jam from her extensive garden allotment, to be sold to profit charities (or give to me) or make the best fudge cake and strawberry pies on the planet. As many as us grandkids will allow her to give away, were indeed donated.

So I was surrounded by strong women who just got on with it. It was all I really knew and that to me was normal. But in retrospect this was not 'normal' and I was quite oblivious to this and carried on regardless, much to the, dare I say, annoyance from other people.

That aside, my painful shyness made me also a great target. I was petrified as a child of somebody cool or god forbid, a boy, saying 'Hi' to me. I knew I would go bright red and nervously stutter something incomprehensible.

Some people do just give off that air of seniority or confidence, those that you do not mess with and that do not give any space or reason to target them. I was not one of those people. I was the geeky kid, who had no idea how to dress cool – apart from my Tom and Jerry jeans, they were a stroke of genius.

In my 20s, I worked at, sometimes failing (who am I kidding – often!), at trying to 'fake it until I made it'. The thing about faking something is that it screams disingenuousness, again making you a target or being unliked. But if you keep at it, it can become a part of who you are.

Combine that with starting to stand up for yourself and form a path that makes you less easy to take advantage of…you will find that when you don't let people disrespect you, they start calling you difficult.

This does make you an excellent target to bring down. To reinstate their assumptions of those that stepped out of their assigned roles. To ridicule and belittle what others are not comfortable with or ready for. A warning 'per se' to those that would consider going against the norms. To vilify women, an act by men to fight to keep a misogynistic way of life that serves them better. Whether conscious or not.

Then I divorced a man that spent in inordinate amount of energy telling people I was a money grabber (the irony), I started seeing a guy whose ex from 3 years ago was still going through a long, calculated and drawn out legal process to extract as much money from him as possible who thought my being on the scene would not let her get away with how she was treating him. A rather well known tricky character who loved a bolshie fight. Despite everyone knowing that they were long since over, she decided to start the rhetoric that I was stopping them reuniting and developed a woman scorned stance, miraculously. Regardless, she was the woman in her 50s, and despite her ex being 10 years her junior, I was the tall blonde younger woman that he was setting up home with.

Cue the tears, the optics were beautifully curated. Aimed to help assist a better financial settlement though coercion and guilt.

Men can do some frightening, egocentric and misogynistic things, but the women, wow they can be vicious.

She and her best friend wanted me run out of town (FFS) and most definitely not to be welcomed at the local rugby club or pubs. So I was harangued and ridiculed.

What surprised me though was how people fear those that can be insidious regardless of the obvious truth. The fear of wanting to be next or going against someone capable of pretty mean behaviour. Even when I was quite publicly thrown drinks on by her and her school teacher friend. Constantly 'accidentally' and drunkenly bumped into and knocked over. To a point where the rugby guys started surrounding me and escorting me to the washroom when I needed to go. Was it well known I was regularly physically being attacked? Yes. Was it stopped? No. Was my husband in on it, standing proudly with them, fuelling the fire? You bet ya.

There was one evening when it got so bad that one of the ex-girlfriend's friends was physically restrained and removed from the venue for being so over the top abusive towards me while my husband and his sister where there with them, by their side. They made a speedy exit when they realised just how much trouble his involvement could get him in. I never spoke to his sister again.

Why did I continue to go? This was my boyfriend's club who he played rugby for. My husband only became a member of the club when I started dating the guy to be the 'thorn in his side', albeit only as a treasurer! It did finally become too much but I originally resisted due to not wanting the bullies to win. Stubborn? Yup. There was also a lot of encouragement from the Chairman of the club to not let them win, as well as long term friends who also attended. The chairman did eventually hold a meeting to discuss what was happening and one of the members (who did play) and who was the partner of the teacher, the ex's best friend, (keep up) was told that he would need to leave. It was decided upon that he needed to somehow get me onside/apologise if this was to be reversed.

He approached me, away from the 'clubhouse' and asked to sit down with me. This resulted in a very weird and boozy night where he tried to explain why he had behaved the way he did, a lot of misconceptions were cleared up. Crazy and ironic tales were told to me about what was really going on and how it all had just escalated and was incredibly fucked up. He also predominantly blamed the women folk.

The diatribe on social media was just as bad. Throw enough mud and some of it will stick. I was a pariah.

All this just sat there bubbling under the surface while I tried to pretend they weren't winning. I didn't have time to break while the divorce was in its final throes.

*

What really affected me, sending me in to quite a downer for some time and indeed so many, was the death of Caroline Flack in Feb 2020. Just how dangerous bullying people and speculating on issues that should be very private can be. Getting involved and having an opinion on events that really shouldn't concern you. Especially when it is very likely you have all or indeed any of the facts. To vilify women, or anyone, because they look like 'fair game'. She was a seemingly confident and pretty presenter, she must be able to take it…Comes with the job, right? Look how successful she is, how much fun her socials show she is having. The life of riley. Bringing her down a peg or two surely couldn't hurt.

Whether it is in high school, in the Daily Mail or in your local pub. It is ALL bullying. Be mindful of what you are a part of and may be contributing to.

Chapter Twelve
Week 12—Asserting Myself

This is something that I have always struggled with. Ironically (considering what I do for a living now), I hugely lacked confidence, I still do but in much different ways/levels now. Horrifically so when I was younger though. Which caused issues as we are socially primed to be accepted, non-confrontational, often by tolerating unwanted and inappropriate behaviour or interactions. Which is more of British thing, definitely in times gone by.

I have definitely tried to address this more, especially of late as my recognition of how limiting and counter-productive such fears and behaviour can affect me and sapping the joy I can take from life. How damaging it can be to relationships if you cannot be honest or feel comfortable. Ultimately what will result is anger and/or deterioration. Either be with people you are comfortable being honest with or take a chance and risk their response if you're unsure. Life is too short to waste on people who don't deserve the real you.

I need to be in control of who I am, as I feel uncomfortable around people at the best of times. If I am not being true to myself than what I'm contributing is a waste of pointless energy that can go elsewhere. I needed to get used to asserting myself more and standing my ground.

You learn a lot about people when they don't get what they want.

This really brought to the fore my boundary/contact issues and helped me to understand why I'm closed off at times.

Being around people I felt comfortable with helped me make informed decisions. I'm chronically awkward and shy which results in me over compensating and saying the weirdest and ridiculous of things. Especially when someone is being nice to me! Let's be honest here, I have a sick sense of humour and I've always felt like I've needed one. My levels of sarcasm have got me in to more trouble than my bad decisions. I was so painfully shy I would ramble nonsense, feign nonchalance or drink to find confidence. Which normally put me in a vulnerable or obnoxious situation.

I was scared to show people how much I needed them for the fear of being ousted or ignored. I was unaware how much I automatically isolate myself to avoid such situations as I had no faith or confidence in what I meant to people. I used to be in awe of people who could show their weaknesses and rubbish sides yet still be loved.

*

One of my mums ex's Paul, who I remained in contact with from the age of 9 after they ended their relationship was a good example of this. Regardless of my reluctance to be with my own dad on his allotted Sunday, every Friday I would have a sleepover at Paul's where we would eat pizza and do code breakers, then he would take me to a horse riding lesson every Saturday morning before dropping me back at home. He was definitely like a second dad that I had chosen.

His parents were people I called in on regularly like any grandparents, they lived across the road from my high school best friend and around the corner form my real grandma.

It started to wane as he found a new partner who had her own child. They welcomed me incredibly and I even holidayed with them. But unfortunately his new wife died tragically of a brain tumour making him the sole carer for the daughter left behind. Elaine's death during my GCSE's rocked me unbelievably so. I would skip classes to see her in her final months and this was my first real experience of death. Seeing that her daughter would be left behind and yet how overwhelmingly contradictorily 'lucky' I thought she was to have Paul that I increasingly did not.

When I moved to London at the age of 19/20, he visited me regularly and took me to dinner. It fit in well with his pension trustee responsibilities in the big smoke. I would say that in the first year alone he visited me more than my own dad and brother combined even to this day.

When I visited Huddersfield, I always prioritised seeing him and his new partner, who would take me to new and more 'middle-class' venues which I loved, and I felt more at ease with considering how disdainful my own brother was with me in his 'local'. This unsurprisingly pissed off my family.

They also visited me near my now 'hometown' of Twickenham, in Kew with my husband for dinner and I felt he engaged with me like family and I mattered.

When I announced I was getting divorced, they asked to see me on my next visit for a pub curry to check in on me which blew my mind. My own family were very blasé, like it was just another 'Hazelism'. Hazel's never happy and just being intolerant. Neither my brother of dad came to see me, even when it got really bad.

During the dinner I explained that I had a good solicitor that would hopefully help me to not let my husband get away with leaving me and the children desolate. Coming across undoubtedly bolshy and they simply responded that I would be fine, "You always are." This cut like a knife and I realised I had been too blasé when what I wanted and needed was support. So I actually explained that I was in fact struggling and quite scared. I'm assuming that this show of vulnerability shocked them and either saw it as bullshit or put them on the back foot of what they expected and panicked them into their actual response. Along the lines of 'Oh Hazel don't give us that, you're the strongest person we know'. I wanted to cry and quickly changed tack to being 'silly me' saying that of course I had it all under control. I made my excuses and left.

I've not really had the same relationships with him since. Contact and effort waned slowly and I'm pretty sure I've not heard from him in the last 5 years. A clear example of any weaknesses I did show being thrown in my face monumentally. So I thought. Realistically it was probably more of a shock to them which determined their response.

*

And yet, my stubbornness is unreal! I can't pretend that things I disagree with are ok. I hate being disingenuous. Much to my friends, my mum's and ex's annoyance! I hate being fake.

Absolutely bonkersly (it's a word) when it comes to other people I care about I am 100% capable of asserting myself and showing up. Why? This is not just me, I'm sure you recognise this in yourself or your friends. We often are incredible for other people and can't seem to find the same strength in our arsenal for ourselves. Is it because we think other people are more worthy? Is there less fear in showing up for someone else?

Another element of asserting ourselves properly is putting ourselves first. Why do we not prioritise ourselves? Why do we fail to source the energy to serve ourselves but happily muster it for others? Mind you, often those that do are vilified for 'being out for no.1'. Even finding the 'acceptable' balance is exhausting.

I remember back in 2020 when I moved in to our new home, the heating thermostat instructions repeatedly got ignored because I couldn't be bothered figuring it out properly. Oh the effort, I'd sort it soon... Then almost 18 months later a friend of mine had moved and was struggling to work through her to-do list and asked me to programme her thermostat – y'know because I'm good at stuff like that. Within minutes, I realised it was the same as mine (glass of champagne in hand) and 20 minutes later it was fully reset and programmed for each day, time and temperature required.

What that actual fuck!

*

I would often get bullied as a kid and just let it happen, hide away and pretend I didn't care. If it happened to a friend, I was stoically by their side offering support, even those I didn't particularly know, as I hate injustice. This can be translated to my modern day relationships too.

Chapter Thirteen
Week 13 – Anger and OCD

This was so clearly evident while talking about what had brought me to counselling. The language I used was so visceral, loaded. Where do I even start? I'm angry about having precious moments ruined. Not being supported. I'm angry that time I could have spent doing something productive was consumed by so much unnecessary nonsense. I'm angry that I didn't have the tools or (seemingly) the time to deal or address my anger, or that I was given the arena and support to do so.

I'm angry that in trying to control my anger, I developed a form of OCD to try and control my environment that I was judged for and even ridiculed. 'Jeez Hazel you are so controlling...' I'm angry that I'm too tired to be a better friend, mother, writer, to look more presentable etc.

I'm angry that in trying to put my children first instead of spending time defending myself I was judged unfairly. I'm angry that I was too ashamed to say how much I was struggling that in trying to hide it, I came across as a very different person. I'm angry that I lacked the skills and confidence to demand the help I needed. I'm angry that I'm too easy to be disregarded. I'm angry that I can't stop being angry.

I was angry that regardless of how much I tried to help other people or even not burden them with my issues, I was angry at how that wasn't recognised. In most cases, this was not anyone's issue other than my own. I had to own it and stop being angry for a situation of my own making.

I was angry that I wasn't allowed to express my sadness and depression over the end of my marriage for fear that I would be persecuted and it would be used against me in court for not 'being capable'. I was angry and embarrassed that my own family couldn't be arsed showing up for me. So I distanced myself further hoping that would help justify it and make it less relevant, less crushing.

I was even actually angry that I couldn't enlist my go-to eating issues to help me with my feeling in control because I knew I couldn't risk being tired and 'hangry' with my children on top of managing everything else. WTAF.

*

Ultimately, I realised from talking to my counsellor that I had sat with the anger of everything and created an environment where I felt very unsafe within myself. I knew I flew off the handle at the kids too easily at the most ridiculous of things, funnily enough the catalyst rarely being in regards to the big stuff. It scared me how quickly I could go from level 3 to level 97 and I became very protective of my surroundings to control this.

Looking back I was clearly suffering with a form of PND, more so after my second child as a result of the issues I faced before getting pregnant, the medical implications that occurred during pregnancy and how they were dealt with. I was so protective of my sanity that I buried it so deeply and it was released in only select ways. Anger and violence towards myself when I was alone, searching desperately for any way of recognition of my own accomplishments to help me 'get by'.

I've used my anger as a propulsion for exercise, I would work out to get rid of excess 'energy'. To work out my fury, anguish and to be able to control something, my weight. News flash, being a mother of 2 who gets her body back quickly does NOT ingratiate you with other mothers. I was alienating myself even further. I was at the gym in the last few days leading up to the day I gave birth to both children and back there within days of giving birth. Why this wasn't a huge siren going off to people in retrospect is boggling! But also, I do know I'm stubborn. Ironically, the better I am feeling within myself, the fatter I am.

The deeper you bury what is happening to you, the bigger the explosion. However, regardless of when that explosion does happen, what you are suppressing will come out in some other way, whether that is varying degrees of control, drinking, anger and dis-ease.

OCD really played a part here. I needed to be organised. I needed to know where everything was so there was nothing adding to my stress 'levels'. I was anxious if I was hitting the gym less that at least 4 times a week. My nappy bags were the most meticulously packed and stocked examples of perfection ever. I would make my husband have his own bag to use when not with me as I couldn't trust him to replenish it to my comfortable standard. I couldn't risk being caught short and the additional potential stress and emergency costs.

Cleanliness was huge. I was scrubbing the floor of my home the night I brought my youngest home. If the floor was dirty, it would just travel through the house and that was way too uncontrollable.

This was also a manic issue with man-thing as he rarely wore anything on his feet when heading out into the garden and then bringing mud/dust/gravel back in. I would plead with him to leave flip flops by the door but he was very forgetful. He is also a grown up and can do what he wants, but I could only relax by either cleaning up after him immediately or by having a drink. Even thinking about it now brings back the claustrophobic feeling of anxiety.

It was a standing joke among my mum friends how I couldn't cope with other people's kids walking in and out in their socks and grubby fingers, unless I was at least a few drinks down. It did used to annoy them until they started to realise it was more deep rooted. It got to a stage that their kids just accepted that Hazel would host, cook and have a laugh but just use wet ones a bit more regularly!

If I was having a particularly anxious time and my levels were getting hard to manage, I would be honest about it and I would be allowed to take over people's kitchen to cook and tidy when I went around. Creating order was like a Ctrl-Alt-Del for me.

It became a bit of a thing that had its benefits. When Hazel was stressed, food was cooked and there was always leftovers! I'm at my happiest when in the kitchen cooking 8 different dishes simultaneously (while maintaining a tidy workspace). This also helped with when I was feeling awkwardly uncomfortable and yet still be a part of being sociable and have people around me, but just busy enough to not be in it too much.

I kind of became a master (pah) at managing that simmering pot and stopping it from boiling over. Excluding myself when I knew my state of mind was beyond engaging these coping mechanisms.

*

I still do this now, but I understand it more. I have rid my life of (most) negative influences or elements that unnecessarily stress me out. I'm kinder to myself in regards to what has got me here – whether that is of my own doing or not. I read A LOT to help understand more about each other, it's incredible how much we think we are on our own. If we were more honest with each other, we would learn so much more and feel less isolated.

I also positively attribute unwanted energy. If I'm stressed, I use it to get my lazy ass off the sofa to run, box, walk, clean, etc. Reframing negativity can work wonders for our mind-set.

A lot of what I discuss above is also covered briefly in Chapter 17 – My Children.

Chapter Fourteen
Week 14 – Me As a Friend, Who Do I Think I Am?

This is the worst and most whingiest chapter for me to write. What is frustrating about depression is the never ending and unstoppable loop of negative thought patterns. I was boring myself with the vitriolic nonsense from me to me.

However, considering everything that we were discussing throughout our sessions and what had happened, we needed to address who I thought I was as a friend to try and understand how I was coping with how my 'friends' had responded to me. How much I do let my friends who want to support me, actually be able to?

Having the time to reflect on this really is invaluable. Who you think you are and how you come across to people are not always aligned.

I do have a default mode to hide when something happens to me, try and deal with it on my own. To try and protect my own sanity until I know what is actually happening, a kind of 'once it's released can it be put back in its box?' situation. I'm very protective to make 'being friends with me' not to be a chore.

One of the main issues with the mental health endemic is based around loneliness, if we open up about our sadness then what does that means for those that say we should 'surround ourselves with positive people'? If we admit we're not feeling positive there is a very real fear of being ousted.

As I previously mentioned, I've never really known where I fit in or struggle with apparently being received properly. I just never really felt that I meant that much to people. So adding to this the fact that I would be a burden made me often want to just be the happy go lucky, jolly and a fun friend. I am quite easy going (or at least I used to be!), which allows people to feel like they can take advantage. It also makes people feel that I take things so easily in my stride, nothing bothers me!

But, I also show my hand too quickly – always have. I thinks it's me being open and genuine when in fact it just opens me up too quickly, too vulnerable with people I don't really know.

Being an empath has also contributed, as discussed in earlier chapters. I know that when faced with a concerned friend who is going through a bad time themselves or who will be quite affected by me relaying honestly what is going on, I just can't do it.

You're friends, real friends want to help. The amount of times I have found out that friends, family and even colleagues have struggled on their own, when I would have loved to help. It's not uncommon for people to not want to be a burden, but we need to start looking at our issues from many angles. Is it worse to not allow our friends the opportunity to care? To leave them thinking that you didn't want them close or seemingly not trust them? It's likely to result in a self-fulfilling prophecy. We really can be our own worst enemies! I have even been known to often unconsciously, test people to see how much they do care. Push them away or use glib behaviour to see what happens. This was really brought to my attention in my counselling sessions and the period after each session when I gave myself time to reflect on what had been discussed.

We/I recognised a pattern of depression/anxiety and focusing on others to distract me. To feed my positivity via increasing other people's. To try and get a natural high from charitable work, caring for someone else...What's wrong with altruism eh?

I have since doubled-down on my honesty in regards to what is going on with me, with people who matter. Those that I know would genuinely be upset to not be kept in the loop, and in return they feel more comfortable to do the same. So much so, that my good friends will often register my lack of usual contact or will know my triggers and be in touch to check in accordingly. As I am with them dependant on what I know is right/preferred.

Actually discussing whatever we may be going through may not always enable us to solve the problem, but airing what is on our mind, as well as processing it with another person can be incredible. Even if we only do it to help them understand why we need space.

*

What really needed to be addressed here and so many of us need to look inwardly at is – Am I as good a friend to myself as I am to other people?

I am that person who will defend my friends arduously. I can be trusted to know where the bodies are buried. Call me when you're stuck, dumped, wanting to put itching powder in your ex's underwear... I'm there to help or provide a narrative that stops you getting arrested and possibly see a better way forward!

I'm a cracking sounding board, so I'm told – even if you don't know me. If you move half way across the world and I promise to be the first to visit, I will. You need inappropriate humour, I'm your girl. A crazy ass night to celebrate or forget something, I am all over it.

When this is not reciprocated, it understandably hurts. But I also need to stop being so sensitive, appreciate people for who they are and make better choices about how to spend energy that is in short supply. We all do.

Are we projecting our own values on to others unjustly and getting upset when people don't respond the way you think you would?

I've spent a lot of time distancing myself to limit how hurt I have got, wondering what it was about me that made me so irrelevant to people. Getting frustrated by history repeating itself. Yet at the same time trying to address my dichotomised behaviour of my empathy and my incredible stubbornness!

Evidently I don't play the game though. I am useless at pretending I like someone who I know is disingenuous, a bully, or if I don't get or agree with people's methods and mentality.

Often being accused of dry sarcasm (I prefer the term wit) or screwing with people who are being openly shit. I hate crappy excuses for bad behaviour, own it. I have so much respect for people who make mistakes (we all make mistakes) but try and make it right, be honest and try and make it better.

Many of my friends and most definitely myself included have done some rather questionable things in our lives but we predominantly own it and are honest. I love this. What I don't like is those that profess to be saintly and claim being 'boring' in comparison through outright dishonesty. That doesn't mean anyone deserves your life story, just that the high horse should remain unmounted.

Chapter Fifteen
Week 15 – My Mistakes

Where do I even start?

As I look back over the years, there are many events and incidents that have formed who I am and the learned behaviour because of them. Many of us have these events both positive and negative that contribute to who we become. Our personalities, support systems, the frequency and prominence of the time of such circumstances affect how much so. Some of us are more susceptible or need to be more protective of our sanity than others.

There is of course the argument of 'well, it always seems to happen to her, there is no smoke without fire'. Indeed, and I do take responsibility for my decisions and situations that I have put myself in. I have made some terrible choices and not just in men, in what I have searched out and my drive to be different or my ill-conceived 'helpfulness' has made me make questionable choices.

I have gone along with things, things I was not comfortable with due to my shyness. I'd had to learn to cover my fear with sarcasm, bluster and feigning stupidity. Often it didn't work!

I went through a stage of feeling guilty about making repeated mistakes, situations repeating themselves. But then I was helped to realise that I was chasing familiar situations. That doesn't mean they are good, just what I know. We do take comfort in familiarity. The unknown is scary, no matter how much we know it is probably better for us.

What I worked on during therapy was discussing ways in which to recognise and therefore not fall into the same patterns of behaviour that has been developed.

1. I've been too apologetic for who I am which gave people an opening to use me as a scapegoat. To project their issues on to me.
2. I've been naïve in my ability to comprehend how I am seen by others and likewise tried too hard to care what others thought which further made me either annoying or an easy target!
3. I have had a pathological need to prove myself or defend certain dubious decisions regardless of how irrelevant it was, or I was.
4. I drink because I'm shy and nervous, but that's also when we behave out of character! Also it has been used to mask pain, or to hide the awkwardness of being an introvert and to make you appear more fun (ergo likeable).
5. Sometimes I let people take advantage of me, just to see if they will. This has become something I do even subconsciously.
6. I pull away from people for fear of further rejection, once initial rejection is sensed. Classic self-sabotaging. I veer towards positively attributing the

worst outcome and manage to convince myself that it's even preferable!

7. In being apprehensive and scared to tell people when I'm upset, it causes destruction anyway due to the way I behave as a defence mechanism and I look like the dick no matter what. I need to woman up.

8. I kept my issues to myself on too many occasions which I understand left me and who I am open to speculation. If you are surrounded by mindful people or those who may understand such behaviour, it is not always as much of an issue. "Surround yourself with like-minded people…"

In my youth, I was an awkwardly shy child. Even now when I see the same traits in my children I try and steer them in another direction or at times force them out of their comfort zone to give them a better chance at not having to face the same challenges I did. Encouraging them to take deep breaths and practise sticking up for themselves when faced with a predicament they don't understand, to feel comfortable with questioning it rather than just shrinking. Shyness often comes across as rudeness or weakness. I know I can be too hard on them at times striving for this.

As a child/teen I was often told that I looked miserable because I didn't smile and to cheer up. Having huge lips always made me quite self-conscious and kids can be very cruel! I rarely knew where I stood. I had been getting unwanted 'advances' from men since a very young age which made me quite insular.

A very disturbing incident when I was 8 at the local swimming baths, retrospectively damaged me and how I felt comfortable interacting with others for many years to come. When you start to fit in, you invariably do whatever is needed to staying 'fitting in'.

In my naïveté, I assumed that incessant attention from men (boys) as much as 6 years older than me at the age of 12+ was down to my incredible maturity. I'd like to say that it was many years ago that I realised I was mis-attributing these scenarios but I have no intention of lying in this book.

Even as I entered my late teens and early 20s regularly employed as a model/actress, which still did not quite boost my genuine confidence in myself – that happened later!

I was told my eyes were my biggest issue, that they made men think they were in with a chance and women hate me for letting them think that. This made me apologetic for years for my problematic eyes which again made me a target, I thought that I was to blame for how people saw me due to my specific actions of not controlling what my eyes did. FFS. Although I must thank the main guy who relentlessly commented and enlightened me to this, it eventually became useful.

Was I to blame? Oh I had my moments. There are the notions that there is promiscuity in those without a positive father-daughter relationship. I was one of those and I did like to have fun, but I know plenty of girlfriends who did not have that as an excuse! As I started to come out of my shell I did like the attention and confidence boost. Men doing this is 'boys will be boys', women are just being manipulative. The 2020s are so much better for women! If you're sexy, you're a threat. Not sexy, dowdy. Great fun, trouble. If you're strong, cold. Financially savvy, must be a gold digger.

Confident, full of herself.

Be a good girl. Shut up. Don't make a fuss. Be humble.

*

Then there was my pregnancies. Get on with it. Constantly making like I was ok with mostly doing it on my own. We kept my first pregnancy a secret only announcing it when I was 6 months gone. We made out like it was nothing, we just wanted to see how long we could keep it a secret. When in reality, I got pregnant way quicker than I thought we would. I panicked as I didn't know him as well as I thought I did and the cracks were showing in those first few months. The control, his self-importance. I was told that the house we were buying would have to have it legally documented that I wouldn't be paying my fair share throughout my maternity leave and his ownership % should represent this.

Due to me buying my first house at 18 in Huddersfield and sold for a good profit, I was financially secure enough to buy my own property. Mortgages were quite easier to get in the early 2000s if you had a decent deposit, oh the good old days! I pointed this out and started my own sole mortgage application, mainly to prove my point. At this stage, we weren't 100% living together and I still shared an apartment with my 2 best friends and spent a couple of nights getting space and panicking at what a pickle I had found myself in. Pregnant with a man's child who clearly was not going to be supportive.

When I went back a few days later, I found dirty knickers in his room and when confronting him about it, I was unceremoniously chucked out to sit in the pub across the road until he calmed down. I couldn't go home as it would be obvious that something had happened and I was embarrassed, especially as it was likely my pregnancy news would soon be coming out.

It was made clear that this was not up for discussion but could we look at £500k properties (carrot dangled) tomorrow to buy together, only documenting the amounts we put in initially as deposits. As I've said, we teach people how to treat us. If we complain, we're awkward. Forgive them, a mug.

*

As previously mentioned, postnatal depression was most likely a huge factor with both pregnancies. Looking back what I did, how I behaved was textbook. But I was convinced I should go with 'mind over matter'. Keep busy, it stops the thinking. Then you inevitably burn out. Rarely do these things pass, they just get buried ready to emerge at another time.

May I remind you, I used to actually drive to my local Sainsbury's car park, drive to the most desolate corner and scream. I was in the gym with both pregnancies until the day before I gave birth and was back within days afterwards. That proves I'm okay and I'm in control, right?

I was constantly crying and frustrated. I remember being exhausted after the birth of my first born, we had moved into our new home at the last minute and I had worked tirelessly to clean and unpack before the birth and then when I was told all my husband's family was descending in days after the birth I would wake in the night and clean. A mixture of nesting and trying to avoid how little control I had over what was happening. My husband's family were sweet but overbearing. Parents, sister and her children arrived and all I wanted to do was sleep and bond with my baby.

His mother did actually see that the situation was 'interesting' to say the least and tried to help with the cleaning, as the kids were excitable and hectic. I remember retreating to my room with Leo for a nap to give him some quiet and I remember telling him that I wish we could just chill and I'm sorry, I wish they would just go home and leave us be... The baby monitor was on downstairs. It has never been mentioned.

Their overbearing nature was a constant battle I faced, especially in regards to the insane amount of clothes and toys that were bought. I wanted a less consumerist way of raising my children, not spoilt or tacky. I was constantly disregarded and ignored. They would wait until I popped out to bring huge sacks of 'goodies' in. I started claiming that I only wanted non plastic toys due to the harm they potentially caused and the space they took up. This was obviously bullshit, I just thought there would be less bought if it was more expensive!

I was repeatedly ignored and not even having 'control' over what my children wore or consumed was hugely damaging to my mental state. Excessive consumerism was a trigger in my OCD.

Even my own wedding I wasn't a consideration for my husband or family. Most brides are very demanding especially when getting married 3 month after giving birth. The great Icelandic ash cloud only just subsided days before the big day! I just got on with it. I didn't want to be a diva or a burden. You teach people how to treat you.

But then again I was not surrounded by mindful people. My own husband chose the location where he could get the most from his BA companion voucher and air miles. He held the purse strings and I was on maternity pay, a whopping

£140pw. This was too far and expensive for my family to afford. My dad, brother and 2 half-sisters did not come. Just my mother and auntie, but a fantastic amount of friends. Ironically predominantly only my friends made the effort to come!

History repeating itself. How can I stand up for myself without putting myself in a situation where I may find out that what I say doesn't matter, or how I am doesn't matter. Don't cause a fuss. So I internalised it all.

*

What is helpful to keep in mind is that some people have experience of certain 'issues' but you may never know. Whether that is through fear, a request/plea from an ex or child for confidentiality, for safety reason or plain old 'my business is my business'. What some people may feel is obstinacy could actually be self-preservation. Unrelenting strength could be their only option. Constant mistakes being made could be the result of a personal turmoil. Stop judging what you may have no entitlement to know.

Paradoxically, if you fear losing something and that fear controls your emotions and behaviour. When you do lose it, does the fear go away? And if so, it that why we self-jeopardise?

If you always do what you've always done, then you'll always get what you've always got. True, but what if you've been doing these things for the wrong people?

Chapter Sixteen
Week 16 – Negative Mental Thought Patterns / Changing My Mindset

All of what we have looked at and scrutinized shows many ways in which I need to change how I think and operate. The issues that brought me to needing counselling clearly had me in some precarious negative mental thought patterns that were annoying me, let alone anyone else. The frustration alone about how I just couldn't 'get over it' or figure out how I had got to where I was, was soul destroying and exhausting. How easy it was to trigger the loop created another level of anxiety causing yet more issues, from OCD to isolation.

Being a victim is a mentality that we can sink into overtime and it is crushingly soul destroying, rendering us less capable of being the best we can be for those that matter, including and most importantly to ourselves.

I have learnt so much about myself and how I have 'operated' for years. I know I never really felt like I fit in, but rather than retreating I've kept myself busy with work, travelling and creating experiences that sound so amazing that they would peak people's interest so I didn't feel so alone.

This meant that as I was working stupid hours, I did well for money. This enabled me to do more and have more independence and freedom. I also wanted to save and ensure that I was never limited in my goals.

This type of thought processing is very damaging and needed changing. I was living my life in a way to impress and feel accepted.

I had developed a need to be loved and seen. There are unfortunately very easy ways to achieve this in the short term, wrong ways and the most unfulfilling ways which cause even further issues.

I had to change my mind set and focus on what I did like about myself, start loving my decisions more. In the process of trying to rationalise and forgive behaviour towards me, I have been searching for all that is bad within me to justify it and therefore accept said behaviour. Paradoxically I have also done the opposite in not being honest about behaviours from others, that have been upsetting looking for positivity in their actions to not cause upset or friction. A kind of ignorance is bliss methodology.

We live in such a fragile state of emotional existence at the moment and it's too easy to project that on to others rather than think open-mindedly. Whether intentional or not. Often when somebody treats you badly, it's not about you. It's an unfortunate outlet for their own frustrations, jealousy and/or anxiety.

I developed a protective mode where I no longer could take any more hurt. I shut out anyone or anything that would potentially destabilise me. I need to assess what it's worth, or work on my strength to cope.

I've never been encouraged (in my incredibly trusty opinion!) to rely on people, therefore the barriers went up and I created a life where I sorted myself out, made plans so I didn't need to rely on people. Petrified of asking for help and being refused, how the refusal or lack of interest would make me feel. Constantly trying to protect myself from that feeling as it scared me, how it affected me.

Don't get me wrong, I've occasionally let it happen, I've trusted and let people in but all I could focus on during this period of my life was those that had let me down. It's like the brain is unable to work any other way. Side note – this is how Selective serotonin reuptake inhibitors (SSRIs) help, aka antidepressants. They try and help you rebuild these pathways in your brain.

Serotonin is a neurotransmitter (a messenger chemical that carries signals between nerve cells in the brain). It's thought to have a good influence on mood, emotion and sleep.
After carrying a message, serotonin is usually reabsorbed by the nerve cells (known as 'reuptake'). SSRIs work by blocking ("inhibiting") reuptake, meaning more serotonin is available to pass further messages between nearby nerve cells.
https://www.nhs.uk/mental-health/talking-therapies-medicine-treatments/medicines-and- psychiatry/ssri-antidepressants/overview/

Yet it can be quite surprising how something so simple can knock you off course. My counsellor and doctor that I was seeing throughout this time in my life, likened how I responded to certain issues as a form of PTSD. Images of people, viewing screenshots of messages, seeing other friends have internal fall outs, experiencing what should be normal 'day to day' arguments, seeing my ex who caused the rift – were all huge triggers that could cause days of being down, panic attacks, retreating to the zombie like state that I had worked very hard to get out of. Oh and the insomnia.

What a cruel bitch insomnia is. No rational thoughts were ever experienced at 3am when you're already overtired. Rendering the next day rubbish as you slept very little, giving even less energy to deal with whatever the day throws at you. You look shit and act shit, so when bedtime comes again, the mind then starts thinking about how shit your day was. Repeat.

What I needed was closure from 'that lot' and what they had supported. The fear and negative though processing loops I was going through and how their lack of consideration towards me affecting what I thought of myself. How being my friend to some was something they had to make excuses for, they were doing me a favour even vaguely keeping in touch. Like I was bringing them down because the stronger willed, agenda fuelled lot were exerting their 'authority' and strengthening this notion.

We judge people on our own standards. What a warped way of the world. But we need to remember this when deciphering who we are and where we belong. I love the phrase, "Never take criticism from people you would never go to for advice."

I needed to change my programming. From a young age, I trivialised my feelings to make others feel comfortable. E.g. Mummy and daddy have split up – its ok we'll see him on Sundays like other divorced parents. I was 3. However, this way of behaving is met with relief or supposed assumption of maturity, maybe even 'easy going'. That's addictive. The feeling that you have made something that is hard for people you love, been made easy.

It can be a hard road making the transition to start showing up for yourself. If people don't like it, what was it that they did like? Are you happy with that?

Chapter Seventeen
Week 17 – My Children

Parenting mainly consists of varying degrees of feeling guilty.

I love being a parent. I love being able to help them learn from my mistakes. I love how ridiculous our sense of humour is towards each other. I love how I have partners in crime to go to amazing places, travel the world and learn about new things with.

I have been torn as to how much I should divulge in this section, as a parent we should always protect our children and yet they are so often the reason we make the choices we do. There are quite a few decisions I made in regards to my old friendship group, romantic relationships and mental well-being related because of my children and their requests, but I won't specify in some instances as to what and who as that would be unfair on them.

I'm very lucky to have been blessed with caring and sensitive children that would be mortified if they thought they had offended or upset someone. They very rarely make demands on who I do spend time with and therefore when any request, whether subtle or not is made, I take it seriously. We're a highly sarcastic and close family with an interesting sense of humour, but it does help differentiate between who we are and are not comfortable with. As a rule, any real objections are discussed in absence of the sarcasm and with such a delicately caring tone that I know it's serious. The more subtle they are, the more hurt/distressed they are feeling and I handle it accordingly.

Remember that what you see on the surface is not always what is really going on if someone is protecting someone else, especially in the case of parents. It is not often anyone else's business why you make the decisions you do. Family matters are just that, not open season for idle gossip.

I see in my children the same nature that resulted in my being taken advantage of or taken for granted in the past. I've tried to encourage and nurture an alternative way to ensure a better way forward for them. Especially in my eldest, he has such similar traits to me and trying to protect him from what he will have to endure if his resilience and ability to assert what is right isn't nurtured. I can be tough with him, people have often noticed/commented, but I want to nurture what I know he is capable of. How our moods are easily persuaded by behaviour that makes us uncomfortable and wanting to protect others above ourselves.

*

When a parent (preferably both) makes the tough decision to end the 'traditional' 2.4 family environment and raise their children separately, this decision is not taken lightly. I understand that some people take a dim view of this, but it is my belief that children thrive in a healthy environment which is rarely conducive to loveless or warring parents under the same roof.

Saying that, even couples that split amicably have differing opinions on what is right and wrong. Children caught in the crossfire of either intended or unconscious sniping/passive aggression against the other. This is not always as easy to avoid, regardless of knowing this is not ok when handling delicate and varying situations that arise. Parents are unfortunately only human too.

There have been many ways the children have been used to get back at me. From guilt trips to the aforementioned passive aggressive 'throwing the cash about' to ensure an air of importance and superiority. Especially when he's let them down or failed to provide emotional support when something crappy is going on with them; "check out my 3rd car/Jet Ski/new games room/new puppy." Or changed their holiday plans last minute to enable him going to a party or due to an abrupt end to a relationship/trouble at home etc. "Hey boys, I'm so rich I bought a new RV." Every bonus he had (post-divorce obvs), the kids knew exactly how much he received. His reluctance to provide the elements of parenting that he didn't enjoy were drowned out with bluster (and tech!). But all on his terms.

I remember the children coming home from a weekend with him and they told me how he had taken them to a pawn shop to sell his wedding ring for £60, they proclaimed that they weren't bothered (clearly by mentioning it?) as they usually did, but were noticeably relieved to know that I still had mine. These things matter and it wasn't an isolated incident where their feeling were just not a consideration of what may not be appropriate. He only had them every other weekend and had more than enough time to pop in on any other day! It started to become a bit of a Joke, sadly.

If I bought them a cracking steak, the next week he bought it in bulk. If I got anything cool, Billy Big Bollocks did it bigger and 'better'. It became a very predictable and at times a fun game. A bit like knob head top trumps. A game my friends and I found hilarious, "Predict his next move get it right and take a drink." I blame him for my champagne habits.

To be honest, the whole delectation to champs was kicked off when I cracked open his very old bottle of Dom P. to have with my beans on toast one night after another late night working/networking with one of his 'resellers and work colleagues'. It became a theme. A bloody tasty one.

If I insisted on what most mothers would assume was a basic right; being in control of their tech usage/knowing where he lived for when they visited/who they were going on holiday with etc. The kids were the ones that suffered through his attitude towards them or me when he didn't get his own way. I invariably gave in (often at their request) or chose my battles very carefully. Much to my friend's annoyance! It was a standing joke that I earned my spousal maintenance. And I used it appropriately – I tried my best, when I could to thoroughly enjoy it.

Men and women are aware of this kind of bullying behaviour from men and still let it or tolerate it happening. If a woman did the same, she would be met with quite a different and demonised response.

*

I have experienced quite a lot of anger and anxiety while raising my children that I felt could have easily been avoided, from the various reasons previously mentioned in this book, to the fear I constantly had of my kids not having anybody positive in their life who would help them with my memory if anything happened to me. I always thought I'd die early and if I did I was petrified that their dad would be their remaining influence. This was hugely influenced by my experience of him and the divorce we were going through.

It did also contribute to me wanting to make my new relationship work beyond what was becoming increasingly unfixable with man-thing. I was desperate to have that familial set up, to have them embedded in something good, to a fault. A set up so solid that if the worst did happen, they may even choose to remain with him. Man-thing was many things that were not ok, but being a step dad was a strength of his.

A lot of anger I felt was through my own frustration of this situation increasingly becoming untenable. My maternal anger was scaring me more and more so. I was exhausted, frustrated, guilt ridden for feeling the aforementioned. I was on edge whenever they were with their dad and who he was letting them be around. He was regularly with the same people that were saying and doing quite cruel things about me and to me, through either spite or misinformation. The kids even heard one of them say something quite shocking regarding something along the lines of 'Ohh I just wish she would just disappear' or a throwaway 'I could kill her'. This to a 7 year old was taken quite literally and resulted in heart-breaking tears and a rather messed up conversation where I had to claim they were my friends and it was a joke. Either way, I am not going anywhere.

Being constantly on edge took me to a place of being near tipping point as status quo, ready to blow my top at any given moment. But I knew that this could even have been intentional, to cause me distress and deem me unfit. So I kept on burying it down, as I describe in chapter 13.

It got to a stage with my ex 'Man-thing', that due to his constant lies, money troubles, issues he was still going through with his ex of which I was regularly on the receiving end of and his stress induced 'false reality' – It caused my levels of anxiety to be at such a level that I couldn't take any more. It was making me incapable of being the parent I needed to be, what they deserved me to be. I was even angry that he didn't see how dangerously all his stress was affecting me, us. I was ashamed of the mother the stress and depression was turning me in to. The shame also resulted in me not imparting to others what I was experiencing, this additional element of why I couldn't sustain this relationship any longer.

Ultimately we need to try and make the best decisions we can and the easiest aren't always the best.

A great book for if you've experienced similar maternal anger/depression and as a result shame, sadness and fear is 'Angry Mother, Assertive Mother' by Cristalle Hayes https://cristallehayestherapy.com/angry-mother

Chapter Eighteen
Week 18 – Jealousy
and Judgement

Oh how damaging it is to care about other people's opinions. But only the lucky few are completely impervious.

Jealousy, judgements, envy are all common and natural human emotions. If anything, it can often show us what we care about. Almost all of us can feel that way, but how we deal with that emotion is a true marker. Envy can be poisonous. But it's what it makes you do, how you treat others that matters.

Sometimes the way we talk about other people is deemed as entertainment, gossip, how people bond over similar ideals. Women and their gossip, eh? But how much is beyond a level of acceptability?

I realised most people treating myself or others like shit is more often than not due to jealousy or persecution. People get annoyed or disgruntled by people choosing a different way to them. It creates a need to defend their own choices or lack of.

The more you love your decisions the less you need others to love them.

How other people have judged my decisions and my misguided need to defend myself has controlled a lot of my behaviour. I have felt the need to put up a solid front to show that I am in control of how I choose to live my life, raise my children, even how I manage my finances. It's ridiculous, I know. But in my mind, the better I am doing the more I thought it would show how less of a car crash I am.

Who was I actually trying to convince? Surely if I show that I'm succeeding that is proof that I'm making good decisions. Right?

Living for the approval of others is toxic and quite frankly a waste of your energy. How much energy I have wasted…

I recall one situation/conversation when I was having it 'explained to me' why people have it in for me. Obviously I was intrigued and welcomed some clarification. One of the girls in the clique had evidently exclaimed, "I always wondered why she had money, that's obviously why!" Then apparently blocked me on any social media we were connected on. She was referring to insinuations from manthing about the lies he created in his head about me (the supposed gold digging, trying to take the house) when he stopped getting what he wanted from me.

No dear, I was brought up in a household with very little money so we were always taught to be cautious with our spending and develop a good working ethic from a young age. I've had a job since I was 12, by age 16 I had 4 jobs all at once. I bought my first house when I was 18 and worked my ass off to make additional payments, only spending what I had. Married young and bought a house with my ex-husband, enabled by the proceeds as both of us had had the foresight to buy young. That property increased as drastically as our marriage failed. I didn't 'rob him blind', in fact I came away with considerably less than I should as I was young and wanted my energy to fight better battles. But that would be crass to put on a t-shirt so people were aware, right?

Also, I have different priorities as a younger mother with 2 children, I focus on my children and home life and safety over many other lifestyle choices. I chose not to spunk my money up the wall on skiing trips, Botox and hair extensions, then complain that it's impossible to get on the property ladder and I most definitely did not get a leg up by my parents. But I shouldn't state that either, as that would be crass also.

*

We've all had those shit mothering days where we feel like we are completely and utterly crap. Failing at the most simplest of mothering duties. Some genuinely quite shit and others a figment of our natural and irrational parental guilt. Imagine that being harshly judged as a sport by every arsehole encouraged to have an opinion?

I did like to give off a carefree stance as that is what those around you would absorb, in addition to a dosage of 'fake it until you make it'. If you get wound up and stressed around your children or because someone had been intentionally cruel, what good does it do? It is counter-productive, so when I was able to stay calm, I would do my best to do so. "Hazel doesn't give a shit about anything, she just takes it all in her stride"—kind of, but predominantly I knew how the alternative would make me spiral. Often I used a good tipple to keep me calm too.

This however became the goal, to quash my spirit. My coping mechanisms were used against me. To bring me down. If I was crushed, then I would be a mess…

PEOPLE WHO ARE INTIMATED BY YOU TALK BAD ABOUT YOU WITH HOPES THAT OTHERS WONT FIND YOU SO APPEALING

*

I'm goofy as fuck with a lazy eye, a family that can't really be arsed with me and divorced before I hit 35. I've had to work hard and from a young age to give myself a leg up. No inheritance or generous aunties. No free childcare or nepotism. So bull shit jealousy excuses are not washing.

I think that's why I gravitate towards people with a form of mental illness, it makes them human, flawed and relatable! Stupidity is not a mental illness though, stupid people I like less so. We know the common themes here, jealousy and unease over resourceful and confident women. I've had it said to me many times that my perceived confidence is why I get treated a certain way. The irony being that I over compensate with false confidence due to being shy! It does unfortunately and unhelpfully makes me appear obnoxious.

WHO HOLDS THE POWER OVER YOUR EMOTIONAL STATE?
Control over our own emotional state? Pah! Why do others have such power over our mental state and general mood? Both in positive and negative ways…

How to win a life:
Step 1. Let people do What they need to do to make them happy, mind your own business and do what you need to do to make you happy.
The end

I can be swayed in the blink of an eye. When it's positive, it's fabulous and indeed that can be self-created. However, in the reverse, it's frustratingly draining. The power that one solitary act of thoughtlessness (or worse), whether intended or not can doom a mood.

We, as human beings are generally social beings and therefore are susceptible to outside influence. More so with the emergence over the last decade of 'social' media. It is not uncommon for those sitting behind technology to seek out those just to hit with venom. It's no doubt an outlet for a much damaged soul, but does that excuse it? I suspect those who have been the recipient of such behaviour would have less compassion.

Just an example of random messages I can get!
This concept has increased in its notoriety and the well
coined phrase of 'In a world where you can be anything, be
kind'. The irony being that those who are most likely to wax
lyrical about such, are those relentlessly on the socials with
a perceived belief in the relevance of their constant
opinions! With little or no thought of the repercussions.
Boredom can be devilish.
The power of negativity; I recall a day recently where
everything went well, kids, hair, interactions while out
walking my dog. I even completed my to-do list and had
some random nice messages from friends and work
colleagues – I'm very lucky to have some great people
around me. It even took me aback, how calm and relaxed I
felt within myself. Then one mean comment on my work,
incensed as it turns out, by jealousy and I slumped. Why did
it matter so much? Why can't it be 'water off a ducks back'?
However, it is very easy to be kind and pleasant. Generally,
it takes considerably more effort and venom to be cruel or
spiteful. That is the difference. Somebody has gone out of
their way to be problematic and intentionally upset you. It's
the motive that is all encompassing.
But, as I would say to anyone else that received such
treatment. Does the opinions of someone that insipid matter,
would you want to be on their wavelength?
I came across a great passage in Lulu Wood's book
'Milkshakes for the Almost Dead':

"No," she says into my hair, hugging me so tightly I think I
might stop breathing, but I don't want her to stop. "No,
Diana, You are loved. And you are exactly the right amount.

Don't pretend to be anything other than yourself to please someone else. If they don't get you, so what? Someone else will. If they don't understand why you care about something, go and talk to somebody else who does. If your passion makes them feel uncomfortable, who cares? You are you, and that is all you should be. And you have to love you. You *have* to."

Yet, bad days happen. We don't all behave perfectly and function as we wish we could or should. Try and think outside the box, put yourself in other people's shoes when you think you have been treated or spoken to unfairly. Compassion can be a wonderful tool. It is harder when they are more frequent, undoubtedly.
But we are stronger than we think. Try compassion and move on.

Chapter Nineteen
Week 19 – Endings

What do you mean, why is this relevant? I naively asked my counsellor. One suspects she may have picked up on a few themes throughout our almost 20 weeks together.

What kind of endings? "Well, let's start with how you will deal with our sessions ending?" Well, yes, I will miss my ritual of attending, then having a mental debrief, on my own with a coffee or a long walk. I really have grown to like these days. But I will have so much more time to get 'stuff' done.

So basically I need to appreciate giving myself self-care time without slipping straight back into 100 miles an hour. "But will you cope? It has been quite traumatic. Where will you go when you struggle?" I suspected saying, "Ah I'll just keep myself busy" was not what she wanted to hear. But it got the topic started.

This really did start a spiralling introspection of how I actually do deal with endings. Oh wow.

*

Moving away was such a default want. Have you ever played that game where you ask yourself a question and you have to answer immediately? No? Maybe just with other people? Well, when I did this my quick answer was nearly always 'I want to leave'. Get out, grab my shit and start again. Learn from my previous mistakes and keep on slogging away until I get it right.

When I left my first high school after the Morecambe incident, I just didn't return one day and never bothered saying good bye to anyone – happy to get out and start afresh. My second high school, which I did really enjoy, I remember my best friend claiming that it was weird how we have spent so much time with each other over the last couple of years and come the end of school I would likely just disappear. I remember being heartbroken at this statement and how it was just expected, and possibly deemed ok. I was watching an episode of 'Saved by the Bell' around this time when they were talking about the end of high school and how heart-breaking it was that this was the end of an era. Keeping in mind that this was not the most serious of programmes, I was in floods of tears about how the end was coming and I was not expected to stick around. Rather than sticking around where I was not wanted/expected, I threw myself into work, modelling (how exciting I should most definitely not miss anyone – distraction, distraction) and leaning on my new work colleagues at Pizza Hut. Which involved plentiful nights out and drinking.

Then on to relationships and the inevitable occurrence of rebound relationships. How I deal with the end of relationships was really brought to the fore. Sabotaging a relationship so it has to end when I'm struggling to pull the plug. As mentioned previously, my lack of ability to be courageous enough to be honest about what is wrong for fear of either sounding pathetic or dealing with their reaction (as previously I have dealt with some rather crazy scenarios), hurting the other person (ironically) or plain old laziness.

And yet I clung on to the idea of my previous friendships to my detriment.

Although, endings for me are quite often a catalyst to get some incredible things sorted and in play. I do thrive under pressure. Rather than accepting sadness, I positively attribute it. I do things just to spite others, because they told me I couldn't. It really serves as a rocket up my bottom. If I could bottle that determination for use anytime, I could be unstoppable!

But there was also the question of how I dealt with the effect of my counselling as it really had helped tremendously. There can't just be nothing. I'm primed to being on edge! But luckily life always has something to throw at you, to keep on flexing your toes.

Endings have typically triggered a period of guilt and yearning to understand my 'failure' and apparent patterns of behaviour. The blurred lines between showing my pain, letting my guard down and knowing who and what matters. Taking care of myself, not just others as a way of distraction.

With the help of my counsellor, and trusting those who genuinely wanted the best for me, I learnt to not feel shame for what man-thing created and did to me. It was misogynistic and riddled with ill-conceived 'good intentions'.

What about the end of my period of depression? Where do I go from here? Once that lid has been opened there is a level of caution instilled to help give ourselves the best chance of not sinking so low again. Interestingly, the label 'PTSD' suggested to me by my counsellor and then confirmed as a factor by my doctor, really helped me.

It helped me to realise why I was getting triggered, rather than getting frustrated about not being able to 'let it go', there was a reason. Therefore I could identify the triggers and see what I could eliminate or work on. It helped me to come to terms with how I'd 'failed' at coping so astronomically. I suppose I would say that it aided closure, an ending.

Acceptance of what did happen, accept it was bad and appreciate what you do have. This is why I had to take myself out of the situation that was triggering me. Not forever, but at least until I felt safe enough within myself. I thought it was a failure on my part which was part of why I couldn't let go for so long, letting go of an adoptive family when I already felt quite estranged. My failure felt like a weakness, but in fact sometimes it takes more strength to walk away from what is holding you back.

Endings often are sad and we can't just bury those feelings. Dealing with sadness and disappointment is something I/we need to learn to deal with in the healthiest way possible. Understand ourselves in the key to doing this effectively.

*

What I can be, is destructive. Self-destructive but all the same it can be quite scary. A kind of 'fuck it' when the shit hits the fan or I'm struggling to cope with an emotion. This is not unique to me by no means I'm sure! But jeez can I drink, party, spend and hit the sarcasm like a bitch.

I am (was?) stupidly petrified of asking for help and being refused—how that would make me feel. Constantly trying to protect myself from that feeling as it scared me to feel that way. I think I have moved gradually away from all sorts of relationships in the past to avoid this...

NOT EVERYONE DESERVES TO KNOW THE REAL YOU.
LET THEM CRITICIZE WHO THEY THINK YOU ARE.

People unfortunately get involved with something they didn't have the experience, facts or emotional capacity to understand. I'm sure we all can be accused of doing this on some level. Judging what we hear in the media, in the school playground, from friends who feel that they have been hard done by. Our opinions affected by jealousy, perspective, pack mentality, fear and 1000's of other possibilities.

It is frustrating, but we have very little control over other people's opinions of us. Solidarity is one thing, bullying is another. Be careful of what you are a part of.

Chapter Twenty
Week 20 –
Understanding Ourselves

And so the end is here.

Understanding ourselves is imperative for growth and leading our best life. No matter how hard your course of therapy is on you. It's a process, one that needs to be completed. What use is half a picture?

We're not perfect, some less so than others and we do stupid things or behave in a certain way that we don't always recognise. Understanding the 'why' is important. This is what I feel I have achieved, mainly.

Our final session served as a kind of 'conclusion'. A look back on what we have discussed and a retrospective discussion on how I feel about what we have uncovered and learnt. It really has been a journey of discovery (still is), understanding and learning to put a few demons to rest.

Resilience

I was convinced I was a resilient person, as did other people, so my complete and utter breakdown was as much as a surprise to me as it was to others. Causing the never ending loop of 'why's', confusion and separation from who I thought I was.

How I am perceived

I've messed up when being proud of what I have achieved, going on about it too much. More as a way of trying to prove I'm not a failure (my issue) rather than 'showboating'. But this has affected how I am received and as a result has affected who people think I am.

How I cause my own problems

Sometimes we want to get caught out doing something out of character to force a conversation, even unwittingly. So much of our behaviour is subconscious that it is scary. Other times depression have disassociated us from caring about the repercussions of our actions or the need to feel something/anything has taken over importance.

I can't control what other people do to me

Me: "But why shouldn't we put people straight when they have false and unnecessary information about us?" – I was emphatically told that it's a waste of my time. People believe what they want to believe. "But it's not fair." – I know, but tough.

"But they wouldn't be so cruel if they knew the truth." – Why do you care? Do you want to be a part of their world?

Counsellor:

"Would you want to change so that you fit into the box they want you in?" – Well, no.

I can't choose the complete and utter nonsense people choose to believe and likewise, they're unlikely the kind of people whose opinion I would want, trust or respect! We are all different, we are not for everyone, but we have to stop wasting our precious time and energy trying to please everyone, especially when they are not interested. I have come across as weak and easy to manipulate because of it. Causing my own problems...

I have let scenarios play out in my head in an all-consuming manner that was just not serving me, it was stopping me from moving on. To an extent, we need to role play and fantasise away our emotions as an outlet. If we keep it all cooped up or buried deep down, it will come back to haunt us. Ignoring what has happened to us forms the path for mental illness. But over consumed thoughts will steal our time away. I read an excellent book once that said when something bad had happened to you and the person responsible would not acknowledge it, nor would they ever, you had to form your own apology and reasoning. This involved three letters all written by yourself. The first a letter explaining why and how they hurt you. The second was a letter as if it had come from them with what you want to hear. The third, a letter to them taking their perspective and compassionately explaining why you understand why they behaved the way that they did.

Get it out, don't bury it and move on.

*

Sometimes the worst thing that you think has happened to you, affords you the opportunity to realise who you are. Not previously needing to or wanting to risk delving into such self-reflection.

The thing is, I wouldn't take any of it back. Funnily enough, the more I understand about myself, the less of a hard time I give myself. We grow from mistakes, we learn more about ourselves and others. I'm less scared, angry and affected by mean judgements. We figure out what is important to us and that is magical.

"You should give a fuck. You really should. But only about things that set your soul on fire and get you to where you wanna be in life. Save your fucks for magical shit."

My wish is for you to find acceptance of yourself and peace. With who you are and what may have happened in the past. To help you understand and increase your awareness of how we react to difficult situations. To also find people that ignite you, accept you and make you feel good about yourself.

We accept a love we think we deserve.

*

A year after my counselling finished, at the side of my son's football pitch one Sunday morning waiting for the game to get going. I was standing with my ex-husband, it was his weekend but on my weekend's off I was still expected (by my son) to show up and I'm all over it. Our new player arrives ready for his debut. His mum turns around. "Ah hi Hazel, how are you?" – my counsellor. This should be a fun match.

We stand as a cosy 3 for the whole match, catching up like old friends and most definitely not mentioning to my ex why we know each other. Because we know we are not allowed to discuss it in such situations, or any situation outside of 'the room'. It would have been weird to ignore each other, wouldn't it? My ex on the other hand just saw a blond mum to show off to. I did feel sorry for him as the bragging and name dropping ensued. As the game comes to an end he quickly gets to his car to make a speedy exit so that she had the time to spot him in his flashy convertible. A standard move at school sports days too!

"That was for you" I state. "I got that," she replies.

As her son approaches he mutters something along the lines of the long commute home as she doesn't drive. I broach the subject discreetly of dropping them off as it is on my way home, understanding that there is a line she has to be careful with. It had been a weird couple of hours as it was, what was 20 minutes more going to do?

That evening I got the professional email from her stating the guidelines of what she can and can't do in regards to past clients and how she will need to behave for future games and training sessions, making sure that if she is less forthcoming it is due to trying to maintain boundaries. I replied saying I completely understand, no post-match vino's and I would offer pick-ups/drop offs as I would anyone else on the main group, like we all did. A ridiculously funny situation, ironically.

How to Move On?

How to move on?

Here's to nearly getting it together, for now...

I have spent a lot of time agonising over how I should be moving forward, what needs to change in light of what I have discovered about myself.

The confusion of people incessantly telling me/you who we are and what we should do. The best thing you can ever give yourself is the gift of knowing who and what you are. What motivates you and what drives you and your feelings.

I need to appreciate my uniqueness, embrace it and accept it's not everyone's cup of tea. People have their own demons to handle and sometimes, just sometimes, you need to leave them to it.

But I do feel I can't win. I want to proceed with my life determining people's actions as irrelevant and move on. But I'm so primed with the trauma and the effects of hiding my grief previously that I now no longer know how to go back to a strong front that in turn alters and furthers your psyche.

Everything is new and constantly evolving.

I have read so much about processing our grief, our past and regrets, however, how do you do that? There's that saying that anger is like taking poison and expecting other person to die from it. But forgiveness is a tricky pill. Do you forgive sexual assault or just try and move on? Do you forgive and put yourself in a situation where you can be walked over again and again? What you tolerate is teaching people how to treat you. Forgiveness is tricky but it can be the only way to get past a stumbling block. I refer back to the book I mentioned that had that great trick to write 3 letters that promote processing forgiveness—even when it isn't wanted.

"Cutting people out of your life doesn't mean you hate them. It means you respect yourself."

What if we could have a whole week of saying what we wanted to anybody with no repercussions? How about cracking open a bottle of wine and writing down this scenario in your head? I bet it's cathartic!

Why do we care so much about other people's negative opinions? Unfortunately, those who are regularly happy to talk badly of others have a heightened sense of their importance and therefore share their opinion widely and loudly. Care less, be better than them.

Care about what matters and take strength in understanding what that is. I'm still practising this. Even earlier today (as I write this) as I was doing a quick spot of shopping after my yoga class, a tad sweaty and definitely not wearing Lululemon. I kept asking myself whether the shop assistants in the 'high-end' shops I went to were wondering if I belonged there. Do I look like their preferred clientele? I had been feeling a tad precious/vulnerable over the last few days and this can make me more self-conscious. But I caught myself and reasoned with how irrelevant that was. Who cares and why would it actually matter? I'll say it again, why would this matter?

I know my truth. I read a book at such a pertinent and shaky time called 'Untamed' by Glennon Doyle. What a cliché to say a book changed me. If I wasn't so happy with what I got from this book, I would admonish myself for being cheesy as hell. However, the section on 'knowing my/our truth' came at such a perfect time that it rocked my soul. I' know who I am and if people want to tell me I'm something else because it suits their agenda and how they see the world, then screw them. That is a battle they have to deal with, not one that should cloud my path or one that I can even change. I'm in charge of my truth and what matters to me, others are not. Nor am I in charge of what should matter to them and what they choose to believe. Life should not be spent dealing with how people want to treat you, which is their problem. Lies and untruths are how some people need to get by, but that is not your battle.

Nobody has the right to lie about you or dim your fucking shine. Feel sorry for them, briefly, and move on.

Ultimately in what you have just read, I have been trying to decipher 'peace' or manage my demons and hopefully the narrative has helped you to do the same. The key to getting us to like ourselves, understanding ourselves. is incredible. We can go on for years and years never really understanding our own motivations.

As I have described scenarios that help explain what led me down certain paths, affected my psyche or helped create the problems facing me, there has been an element of poetic licence to protect certain people, their vulnerabilities and families. But only when this has no effect on the integrity of what I am explaining.

What has been problematic, is going over and writing about things that have happened in my past that have been traumatic. At times, bizarrely cathartic (I have used this word so much it must be true) which is nice, but at other times I have had to delay writing to protect my mind-set. Prevent overload and being overwhelmed with the past and yet ironically at times when I have been doing well and really feeling positive and at ease with myself – I've not wanted to kill that buzz!

Remember, sometimes you do just need a good cry though, to let out what you have been keeping in. It's not weak or defeatist. What it can be is cathartic (again), a release, self-care and acceptance that you are experiencing emotions that need to be acknowledged and not buried.

If this book helps even just one person rationalise their behaviour or behaviour towards them, then it's worth it. Those who struggle with mental illness and in attempts to bury the issues or avoid areas of difficulty have only made things worse for themselves and the mistakes that then ensue because of that.

To help people fit in, who have felt they are not enough or too much. Tackling issues of misogyny, jealousy, bullying and abuse.

I now know who I am. Do you?

You are not for everyone.
The world is filled with people who, no matter what you do,
will point blank not like you. But it is also filled with those
who will love you fiercely. They are your people.

You are not for everyone and that's OK.
Talk to people who can hear you.
Don't waste your precious time and gifts trying to convince
them of your value, they won't ever want what you're
selling. Don't convince them to walk alongside of you.
You'll be wasting both your time and theirs and will likely
inflict unnecessarily wounds, which will take precious time
to heal.
You are not for them and they are not for you; politely wave
them on, and continue along your way. Sharing your path
with someone is a sacred gift; don't cheapen this gift by
rolling yours in the wrong direction.
Keep facing your true north.

Rebecca Campbell.

Covid-19 Quarantine

Bizarrely, covid gave me the time I so longed for to write this book but when it came to it, I just couldn't. Quarantine gave me too much time to think, dangerously so. It dawned on me like a thunderbolt just how low I was and wow how weird it was to comprehend my overwhelmingly reflective brain patterns. It was all too raw. Oh the irony of wanting time to check out and write, but being unable to utilise it!

On top of this, we had the panic initially of wondering if our jobs were safe, scared of catching 'it', home-schooling and isolation anxiety. Whereas before when I could write, it would be away from home (and my children) in a cafe or bar where I could separate myself and then have time to decompress before I went home in case I was a bit overwhelmed. This was no longer an option and I didn't want to risk putting added pressure on our home life – making it easier for me to 'lose it'.

This book was very hard to write anyway and took its time due to the effect of re-living certain events, the strain of Covid and additional events life can throw at us. Even sourcing certain screen shots or researching accurate timelines that brought up re-reading messages that triggered my PTSD. As I got better, at least knowing that I had to at least do it away from home or when the kids had gone to bed as I knew it would put me on edge.

Writing can be a double-edged sword. On the one hand, it can help order our thoughts and rationalise, help decipher meaning, very much so like self-therapy. Yet it does, in cases such as this book dredge up old wounds.

During the 2 years of the pandemic, in regards to my 'Get Booked' show at Women's Radio Station (and soon after, additionally Men's Radio Station too due to its success) I was incredibly inundated with all the 'Indie' writers finally managing to bash out 'that book' they finally had time to write. I loved how busy I was and the incredible books I got to read, but it did smart a bit that I was the opposite!

THE WOMAN WHO FOLLOWS THE CROWD WILL USUALLY GO NO FURTHER THAN THE CROWD. THE WOMAN WHO WALKS ALONE IS LIKELY TO FIND HERSELF IN PLACES NO ONE HAS BEEN BEFORE. ALBERT EINSTEIN.

For more information on my literature focused mental health awareness work, check out my radio show 'Get Booked' at WomensRadioStation.com or on my website HazelButterfield.com

WHY I STARTED 'GET BOOKED'

There are many reasons that I have reading and writing as a top priority in my life. Writing for a start is cathartic and allows me to unjumble what is going on in my head and share with others something that hopefully may help them or even entertain them. Reading is a chance to escape, learn something new, increase empathy, be a distraction and/or keep you off tech!

I've always been a reading and writing fan. I was that kid in the local paper who was being reported on for reading way above my age (and excessively!).

I'm not the first person to be overwhelmed by life's circumstances and I definitely won't be the last. However, it got to state where I could not stop over-thinking about a

particular life event that was causing me huge distress. It would keep me awake for hours at night and break my mood instantly. I couldn't concentrate. I was getting angry at myself as well as others for the time it consumed. The more I thought about the situation the more prominence it took, which it did not deserve. I had to switch things up. I needed to retrain my brain.

It took a while, I could get 3 or 4 pages along and realise that not a word had sunk in. I had to retrain my focus, but I needed a reason other than somebody telling me to 'snap out of it'.

So I started a show at Women's Radio Station all about books, authors and writing in general. This not only forced me to keep to deadlines (being ready for the interview with the author) but the onus was on not letting somebody else down—as we rarely try and look out for no.1 first! The more I read, the better my understanding of the story being told— which resulted in a good interview. The praise I was getting both from listeners and the authors started to drown out the negativity of the aforementioned situation that I had found myself in.

This also then meant that I was building a network of authors and bloggers who wanted to come on the show and chat about their journey. Women's Radio Station has a fantastic and clear focus on Mental Health and Well-being which contributed to the ethos of my interviews and furthermore the genre of books I reviewed. My experience gave me a greater understanding of the topics discussed but unfortunately it could also ignite feelings I was trying to stop being overwhelmed by. But ultimately it was worth it and like therapy in itself.

I'm a big fan of positive attribution, no matter what happens I like to find the positive angle in anything. If I hadn't have gone through what I did, I'm not sure I wouldn't have had the introspective ability I now have to produce the 'Get Booked' interviews that I do. To get to meet the incredible authors and writers out there, some of which I now class as good friends and/or have been a delight to have had on my journey.

'Get Booked' is my show on Women's Radio Station where we talk about what I've read, what I'm reading, new releases, chat to authors, bloggers, publishers and book enthusiasts. All based around supporting women's emotional well-being, opening discussions and offering support via the incredible writing community out there.

Come and join us, get involved and if you want to catch up on previous shows you can at https://womensradiostation.com/shows/get-booked/ or on our SoundCloud.

Related Blogs

What is happening with men at the moment?
https://vocal.media/humans/what-is-happening-with-men-at-
the-moment

There appears to be movement of women being fed up with men. Unacceptable behaviour from certain men and the absolute shock as to why this is happening too frequently to women.

It's like they are trying to find a way to exert their authority over women, maybe through not knowing an ever

198

changing role, whether subconsciously or not. Testing the boundaries of human decency and acceptability in a world where 'we can't seem to do or say anything anymore'.

Men are bullying women who don't fit into their box of what they deem acceptable or to get their own way whether it's financial or socially, scaring women into getting back in said box by threatening their family lives and security. I had a date once brag to me about how he earned more money and was therefore able to screw his wife over in the divorce with a better legal team. It was a great look.

Independence in women is scaring some men and affecting their self-esteem.

Those men whose advances you may have turned down, those who don't understand you and then form an agenda to degrade you. A case of 'throw enough mud' eh? Shame women into not being able to stand up for themselves. If a woman hits back, she is being aggressive...

I've had a 'friend' asking if I would be interested in having an affair behind his wife's back, because, you know I'm single. I point blank refused and was surprised to hear it was common knowledge among his close friends that he'd asked me. Apparently it was ok, it's just him, and he's a terror. If a woman did that to a man, she would be run out of town with the proverbial pitchfork and forever labelled a harlot (or your preferred name).

I have been subjected to an ex-boyfriend not letting me back in a home we shared (mid-process of us moving out) after chasing me out after he came home drunk and having one of his 'episodes', until I squeezed past him in his underwear. Witnessed by his friends, worried as they were but no repercussions.

One ex actually wanked on me while I was asleep, I'd woken just as he was finishing and struck by shock, disgust and fear sat with shame for days until I confronted him. Not only did I not get an apology, I got told that it wasn't his decision to split up and (I quote) "blaming him will not help if I want to remain friends." Funnily enough that was not on my agenda. Primo gas lighting.

Friends of mine on dating sites tell me they're told there are a prude if they don't return sexual advances or ghosted if the messaging doesn't sound like they're on a promise. Telling me that 99% of exchanges are about sex.

Don't get me wrong, I like banter and even inappropriate humour. I'm the first to appreciate a blue waffle gag and I'm definitely not a 'prude'. But guys, be better. We all have responsibility in regard to what we are tolerating.

I know someone who actually degraded his girlfriend's physical appearance among all of their friends to score points over a messed up misogynistic agenda. Why were these supposed friends tolerating this? Were pack rules more important?

But shockingly, and worryingly I don't think these men's egos even think it's an issue anymore. They are primed to thinking they are untouchable and it's acceptable.

We all have a responsibility to each other and the future well-being of our friends, children, nieces, nephews and people you may never even come across. "Oh that's just the way he is," is not acceptable. Covid isn't the only pandemic infecting our communities. Please be aware of what you are a part of, even tolerating certain behaviour makes you complicit.

To the men that this applies to, whatever messed up nonsense you tell yourself to justify your actions, think, if this happened to your daughter, would you be ok with it? If the answer is no, than there is a good chance you're being a perverted misogynistic knobwaffle.

More at:

https://vocal.media/authors/hazel-butterfield

Book Recommendations

Shine Brighter Everyday – Danah Mor

"And I realised that I actually see much more than many people. I realised just because we have ears, it doesn't mean we listen, and just because we have eyesight, it doesn't mean we look." This book is going to change my life, for the better. What Danah Mor brings to the table (quite literally) is common sense science and advice in such a beautiful book that I'm actually excited to start living and eating more mindfully. It's one of those books that you not only want to keep out on show, but talk about with your friends to spread the word. From rats showing us that sugar is more addictive than cocaine, to how the best food for us simple, cheap and fun to propagate. Throw in chemical induced cows, to understanding our receptors. Ooh and delicious recipes!

Incredible.

Untamed – Glennon Doyle

What a cliché to say a book changed me. If I wasn't so happy with what I got from this book, I would admonish myself for being cheesy as hell. However, the section on 'knowing my/our truth' came at such a perfect time that it rocked my soul. I know who I am and if people want to tell me I'm something else because it suits their agenda and how they see the world, then screw them. That is a battle they have to deal with, not one that should cloud my path or one that I can even change. I'm in charge of my truth and what matters to me, others are not. Nor am I in charge of what should matter to them and what they choose to believe. Life should not be spent dealing with how people want to treat you, which is their problem. Lies and untruths are how some people need to get by, but that is not your battle.

This book is full of chapters that you want to share with your friends or spur you on to write a sycophantic yet well-meaning tweet. It's honest, fun and unapologetic and the way Glennon can break down preconceived agendas and thought processes is so uplifting.

How To Grieve Like A Champ – Lianna Champ

This is a beautiful and intricately written book for anyone who has lost somebody, has tried to support someone through a loss or will lose somebody. So that is all of us. How to grieve like a champ is so obviously written by someone who's calling it was to support people in times of bereavement and help people through the grieving minefield. Lianna's dedicated work as a funeral director, a role she knew was for her since her teens and from her experience of such has also become a grief counsellor, aims to help people to live not just survive following a loss.

Listen in to my interview with Lianna on 'Get Booked' at Women's Radio Station in the New Year.

'They' say you shouldn't judge a book by its cover, but I guess in this case we can. The narrative is just as enticing as you want it to be. Snappy short chapters, nailing the complexities and intricacies of teenage and adult life and mental well-being. Throw in some ball achingly wealth centred misogyny, unrequited love and jealousy, just wow. There are so many poignant conversations and unapologetically strong female characters, that I just loved it. I still don't know if this is for late teens or adults, but I don't care!

"There is a special place in hell for women who don't support other women."

FAR FROM WHAT I ONCE WAS BUT NOT YET WHAT I AM GOING TO BE.